Alan Butler has been a prof[essional writer for] decades. History is his lifelong obsession, and he has travelled the world, often asking questions other historians ignore. With a start in life as an engineer, Alan is also a musician, a frequent broadcaster, a writer and director of plays for stage and radio and claims to have a curiosity the size of a planet.

John Ritchie has enjoyed an often exciting career as a much-travelled film and stills cameraman. Now based at his home in Scotland, he is a writer, a regular broadcaster, a frequent contributor to documentaries, co-owner of several world-famous web sites and, most importantly, an historical researcher. He has an unparalleled knowledge of Rosslyn Chapel that extends back to childhood.

Also by Alan Butler
The Bronze Age Computer Disc
The Warriors and the Bankers
The Templar Continuum
The Goddess, the Grail and the Lodge
City of the Goddess
How to Read Prehistoric Monuments
Intervention

with John Ritchie
Rosslyn Revealed

with Christopher Knight
Civilization One
Who Built the Moon?
The Hiram Key Revisited
Before the Pyramids

ROSSLYN CHAPEL DECODED

New Interpretations of a Gothic Enigma

ALAN BUTLER & JOHN RITCHIE

WATKINS

Sharing Wisdom Since 1893

This edition first published in the UK and USA 2013 by
Watkins, an imprint of Watkins Media Limited
Unit 11, Shepperton House, 89–93 Shepperton Road, London N1 3DF

enquiries@watkinspublishing.com

3 5 7 9 10 8 6 4

Designed by Jerry Goldie

Printed and bound in the United Kingdom by Tj International Ltd,
Cornwall, Padstow

A CIP record for this book is available from the British Library

ISBN: 978-1-78028-492-7

www.watkinspublishing.com

Contents

Acknowledgements   vii

List of Figures   ix

List of Plates   ix

ONE – The Chapel on the Glen   1

TWO – In Search of a Saint   17

THREE – The Bones of the Holy   34

FOUR – In Dangerous Times   53

FIVE – Renaissance Men   68

SIX – A View to the East   87

SEVEN – The Blood-Red Light   105

EIGHT – Peeling Back the Layers   127

NINE – Into the Forest   146

TEN – Christianity's Cousin   158

ELEVEN – In the Crypt   177

TWELVE – The View to the West   195

THIRTEEN – The Judaic Connections   215

FOURTEEN – The Chapel Then and Now   229

APPENDIX – Extract from 'Acts and Martyrdom of St Matthew the Apostle'   245

Notes   251

Index   254

ACKNOWLEDGEMENTS

It is always difficult to thank everyone for their input. There is a wealth of people who helped us in all manner of ways, as well as those who offered discussion and advice on the subject of early religion and Rosslyn. Unfortunately, there are too many individuals to list here, but to all of them we offer our profound thanks.

However, we would never have been able to complete this book without the support of our partners and families. We wish to offer special thanks to Kate Butler and to Catriona and Hynde Ritchie. Their patience, understanding and support have been the stuff of legend.

We also wish to offer a special thanks to all the excellent guides and staff at Rosslyn Chapel for their forbearance and assistance throughout our years of research, especially Colin Glynn-Percy, Simon Beattie and the evergreen Nancy Bruce. Included in our appreciation is The Rosslyn Chapel Trust, and Lady Helen Rosslyn, whose love for the building has been the driving force behind its renaissance and the wonderful restoration that has secured its wellbeing for generations to come. Our thanks also go to the restoration team and particularly to stonemasons like Iain Bennett who shared many of their finds with us, giving us a depth of knowledge we did not previously possess.

Thanks must also go to Pat Napier, the amazing lady who always finds obscure texts, and to Dr Robert Feather for his incredible knowledge of early Egypt and Qumran which he is always willing to share; to Brenda Franey for being Brenda Franey, to Iain Grimston, Robert Brydon and Douglas Ritchie, who were always ready to give their very welcome and informed opinions, and to Mr Scott Grant for his technical knowhow.

Special thanks also go to the founders of the Saunière Society, Joy and the late John Millar, who have encouraged many authors in their pursuit of answers to the Mysteries; to the wonderful Henry Lincoln, whose ready support is always much appreciated, and to Dr Jonathan A Glenn for his incredible translations of Gilbert Hayee's prose works.

We also offer our thanks and appreciation to the people of Roslin village and to the late George Campbell of the Roslin historical society.

Finally, but most sincerely, we thank Sir William Sinclair, Earl of Rosslyn, and Sir Gilbert Hayee, who left us such a wonderful treasure and the most fascinating series of historical paths to follow.

As far as the book itself is concerned, grateful thanks must go to Michael Mann at Watkins Publishing and particularly to Shelagh Boyd, our editor, who always makes what can so easily be a chore into a pleasure.

LIST OF FIGURES

1 Ground plan of Rosslyn Chapel (▲)   2
2 Cubes carved into the arches of the Lady Chapel (‡)   6
3 The extension of the retrochoir beyond the great east
   window (Δ)   99
4 The roof path on the southern side (Δ)   103
5 Seats at the east end of the Chapel (‡)   105
6 Rosslyn light box (‡)   113
7 Early 19th-century photograph of the ruined east
   window (◆)   117
8 Agnus Dei from Piece Hall, Halifax, Yorkshire (Δ)   188
9 'Wine is Strong' inscription (‡)   217

LIST OF PLATES

1 View of Rosslyn Chapel in the 1860s, taken from
   Rosslyn Glen (◆)
2 The angel of St Matthew with an open book (‡)
3 Photograph of the Apprentice/Prince's Pillar (‡)
4 Tetrahedron of Gordian knots at the top of the middle
   pillar (‡)
5 Interior of the Chapel (‡)
6 The pinnacle beehive (‡)
7 A depiction of Enea Piccolomini, Pope Pius II (‡)
8 View from east end showing 'notch' in the hills (‡)
9 Observatory platform looking north (▲)
10 Exterior detail showing the lower roofline of Rosslyn
   Chapel (‡)
11 Retrochoir showing observatory (‡)
12 Early photograph of the east end of the Chapel (◆)
13 Rosslyn Chapel ceiling (‡)

14 Demonstration of the light box illuminated (‡)

15 Light box seen from the interior with blood-red light (‡)

16 A typical Green Man (Δ)

17 Green Man carving in a niche behind a statue (‡)

18 King Darius carving from the east end of the Chapel (‡)

19 Agnus Dei carving (‡)

20 Statue, believed to be of St Matthew, with scroll (‡)

(‡) Courtesy of John Ritchie

(▲) Courtesy of Alan Butler and John Ritchie

(Δ) Courtesy of Alan Butler

(♦) Courtesy of the Hill and Adams Collection

CHAPTER ONE

The Chapel on the Glen

I n 2006, a film version of Dan Brown's blockbuster bestseller *The Da Vinci Code* was released. The film turned out to be even more successful than the book, and for a while this proved to be an unbelievable boon to what previously may have seemed to be the least likely international tourist attraction.

Set as it is in the lovely countryside of Midlothian, Scotland, Rosslyn Chapel was certainly not unknown and was already receiving upwards of 30,000 visitors a year. But once the film crews had packed up and gone and *The Da Vinci Code* exploded onto cinema screens all over the world, for a while this incredible little Gothic masterpiece saw 180,000 people passing through its turnstiles per annum; on some Sunday afternoons as many as 1,000 visitors arrived at the small chapel.

If you have not yet driven down the short track from Roslin village, just 8.5 miles from Scotland's majestic capital city of Edinburgh, you have missed what many people have described as a genuinely significant moment in their lives. We have been there countless times, and when listening to those who had

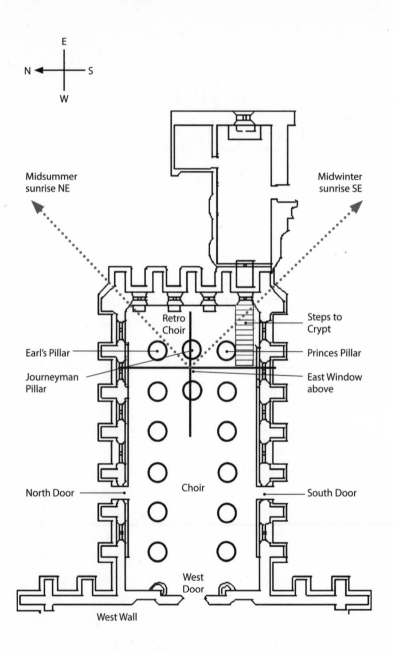

1. Ground plan of Rosslyn Chapel

recently arrived, we have nearly always encountered the same reaction.

"Isn't it small?" they say as they stand at the visitor entrance and gaze at the pinnacles and buttresses, "I somehow expected something much larger!"

After this, newcomers walk along the path and enter the south door, passing into the cool interior. There is almost always a short delay, whilst eyes adjust to the change in light, which is invariably followed by an exclamation in any one of a hundred or more languages that have reverberated around this old and hallowed space in recent decades.

If Rosslyn Chapel had a consciousness, it would doubtless be astonished at its change of fortunes at the end of the 20th century and the beginning of the 21st. For 300 years the building stood, broadly unappreciated and forlorn, threatening to become yet another stately ruin on the British landscape until William Wordsworth and his sister brought it to the attention of Queen Victoria and her husband Albert, who were captivated by a Scottish romanticism they had helped recreate. Their royal interest ensured that Rosslyn Chapel would be rescued and fully restored eventually.

It matters little how many times one has visited Rosslyn Chapel – it never fails to inspire a sense of incredulity and wonder. Inside and out it is a confection in stone – a demonstration of the master carver's art that is unrivalled anywhere in the world by more famous and much larger buildings. Here, in this comparatively remote spot, in a windswept country, clinging to the edge of Europe, someone glimpsed paradise and found the means to translate their dream into a three-dimensional portrait.

In its architectural style Rosslyn Chapel is not so different from other churches that were being created in the 15th century. It represents perhaps the greatest flourish of the Gothic, a style that had first appeared in the 12th century, but which had grown mature and confident across 300 years. The Chapel is a perfect miniature, with all the details one might expect to find at Notre Dame in Paris or at Rouen in Normandy, though presented on a more human and approachable scale.

According to tradition it took around 40 years for Rosslyn Chapel to be completed, and when one has had the chance to study its many facets in detail, this does not seem likely to be a groundless boast. Much of the interior of the building was used as a canvas for the stone carver's art. For example, the full length of the barrel-vaulted roof is a mass of stars in relief – and it is worth mentioning that, when first completed, these would have stood out as silver in a sea of blue because all of the carvings were once resplendent in vivid colours.

Nevertheless, the eyes of all visitors are drawn immediately to the eastern end of the building, where a complex interweaving of superbly carved and decorated arches stand guard over the retrochoir and the altar – if indeed altar is the right word in the case of this incredible structure. The faces of glaring green men, with their foliate ornamentation, peep out from bosses, and angels hang precariously all around – each unique and perfect. Three magnificently executed pillars stand guard over the eastern end. The northernmost of these pillars, known alternatively as the Prince's Pillar or the Apprentice Pillar, is the most wonderful of all. It is a fluted column, but wrapped around with spiralling vines, which, at the top of the pillar, explode into an orchard or a mystical garden, frozen in stone.

All manner of branches, each carrying finely carved leaves and superbly detailed fruits, create a serpentine path down the north wall of the Chapel. In truth, it is difficult to take it all in. John has lived in this place for his whole life and has been in the Chapel thousands of times, but he still regularly finds details that he has never seen before amongst the carefully ordered chaos.

There are scenes of everyday life, with dancers and musicians, as well as a gruesome 'dance of death'. Strange masks, depicting long-dead, semi-mythical characters from the Old Testament vie with grotesques of every conceivable sort, and throughout this end, arches are covered in mysterious little stone cubes, the faces of which all carry unique and delicately handled designs.

When the whole truly theatrical spectacle was picked out in the bright colours that present-day conservators can be certain were originally used, to stand in this place would have been to inhabit an enchanted forest, like a vivid memory of a dream – or perhaps in some cases a nightmare.

The true wonder of Rosslyn Chapel does not simply come from an appreciation of its splendour, together with the knowledge of how much work went into it, but rather from a sense of puzzlement that it should ever have been created at all. Rosslyn Chapel is no cathedral, and was never intended to be one. It isn't even a conventional parish church in the general sense of the word. It is a private chapel, built exclusively by one man for the use of his own family and those who lived in the village he had also created. It was the sort of foundation known as a 'collegiate church'. Such establishments were named after the

2. Cubes carved into the arches of the Lady Chapel

'college' that attended and ran them. The college consisted of four to six ordained priests or prebendaries together with a number of choristers. The men, also known as canons, were not monks, but rather lived in the community. It was their job to sing masses for the souls of the patron's family – in this case the Sinclairs – to officiate at daily services, weddings, funerals and baptisms and to generally look after the foundation.

Earl William Sinclair

The man who was responsible for Rosslyn Chapel was William Sinclair, Earl of Caithness, Baron of Roslin and, until 1471, third Earl of Orkney. He was born in 1410 into an influential family of Norman French origin, but one that had already been in Scotland for a protracted period. William's grandfather, Henry Sinclair, had been first Earl of Orkney, a staunch defender of the Scottish Crown and a great seafarer, whilst his father, another Henry, had continued the life of service to the Scottish kings.

There can be no doubt that William Sinclair was wealthy. He owned vast swathes of land in Scotland, but he became richer still when, in 1455, he exchanged his Orkney earldom for the lands of Caithness. Then, in 1456, he sold the extensive Douglas lands of Nithsdale inherited from his first wife, Elizabeth Douglas, to the Scottish king. From all this acquired wealth he was able to build Rosslyn Chapel. And to assist matters, in 1471, he received land in Ravenscraig in Fife as well as a significant cash settlement as the final payment for Orkney.

Some of this money undoubtedly found its way into the later stages of the building and ornamentation of the Chapel. The building as we more or less see it today took 40 years to finish, but William had a long life by the standards of his times and he did not die until 1484 – though in the estimation of some researchers into Rosslyn Chapel, he still did not see the end of his project.

It is ostensibly clear that what we see of Rosslyn Chapel today was only the east end of what was intended to be a cruciform building that would have extended much further to the west. The masonry at the western end of the building appears to end in a ragged manner, as if merely waiting for the remainder of the church to be built. Whilst researching their book *The Hiram Key*,[1] writers Christopher Knight and Robert Lomas sought the advice of architectural experts regarding the apparently unfinished structure. The experts told them that, in their opinion, the fact that Rosslyn Chapel was ever intended to be any bigger was a fiction. Although it had been deliberately made to look like a truncated part of something bigger, the hanging stonework was a 'folly'.

They considered that the same was true in the case of the supposed footings or foundations for the remainder of the church, which explorative archaeology showed to be below the turf at the western end. In the opinion of the architectural experts, such footings could never have supported the supposed structure they would have had to bear.

The building we see today was the third of three religious foundations in the vicinity, created by the Sinclair family. Originally, the family, and probably locals too, had worshipped in a chapel that was part of the nearby Rosslyn Castle, home of the Sinclairs. At some stage, another chapel was created. You can still see a crumbling remnant of this building in the burial ground, adjacent to the present Chapel. Both the old chapel and the present one carried the same dedication – to St Matthew the Apostle and Gospel writer. The dedication of the site to this particular saint turned out to be one of the most significant factors in our research, as we will show in due course.

The Protestant Reformation

At the time the Chapel was built, Scotland, and indeed the whole of Western Europe, was Catholic. This was not a state of affairs that would last for long, after the final carving was finished and painted. From the beginning of the 16th century, in various places across Western Europe, calls were being made for wholesale changes in the way the Church was run. Popes, cardinals, bishops and priests were being accused of corruption, vice and behaviour that was anathema to their supposed spiritual calling. The influence of the Renaissance on education, greater literacy and new moral imperatives were all adding to an atmosphere in which Protestantism began to appear.

At first slowly, but then gaining ground, reformation began to take place in countries on the Continent. In England, to Scotland's southern border, Henry VIII eventually broke with Rome, and although his new English Church was still inherently Catholic, Protestant sympathies were growing in strength. Finally, in 1560, Catholic worship in Scotland was banned, and the whole Scottish Church was reformed along Protestant lines.

One of the greatest complaints against the Catholic Church had been its wealth and opulence, which many saw as being counter to the teachings of Christianity. In both England and Scotland, popular gatherings and state-sponsored commissions sought to strip Catholic churches of their wealth. Relics, in the form of the bones and possessions of saints, fell completely out of favour, and a new, far more austere form of church interior became the norm. Wholesale vandalism was common, with many fine church interiors being completely smashed, their gold and silver robbed and their relics discarded.

Buildings such as Rosslyn Chapel – and indeed *especially* Rosslyn Chapel – became an anachronism. There were people around who would willingly have preserved such ornamentation for its own artistic sake, but such individuals were in the minority, and if they had spoken out, there was a danger they would be accused of being Papists, with the awful consequences that followed.

How Rosslyn Chapel survived this period of frenzied smashing and burning is something of a mystery. We do hear tales of brave individuals rescuing the Chapel by diverting angry mobs to other locations, and the Sinclairs too helped by encouraging Protestant services (most notably a baptism of Simon Sinclair's children conducted by the brother of the infamous John Knox) to take place within the Chapel. All the same, it is a near miracle that a building so obviously dripping with statuary and apparently religious icons survived, more or less, intact. True, many of the removable statues have disappeared from their niches, but the most wonderful of the fixed carvings, save for the ravages of time and weather, remain as they always were.

Somewhat isolated, and probably still loved for its beauty if not its apparent religious foundation, Rosslyn Chapel slept away the decades. The fact that it was on private land would have helped. The Sinclair family and then the Erskine-Sinclairs still held great sway in the district. They remained significant and powerful landowners. Doubtless, Rosslyn Chapel became something of a romantic ruin, especially when such things were so popular in the 18th century. The family still lived in part of Rosslyn Castle, so this fine Gothic masterpiece – now apparently divested of its religious significance, was virtually in their garden. Poets visited the Chapel, and William Wordsworth himself wrote a poem – *Composed in Roslin Chapel During A Storm* – about his experience there during a thunderstorm.

Some effort had been made to keep out the weather. In 1736, Sir James Sinclair had glazed the windows of the Chapel, though this is unlikely to have included the great east window, which was open and without glazing in 1843. However, he also put flagstones on the floor of the Chapel and had the roof repaired.

We can tell from very early photographs taken by Hill and Adamson that the Chapel was in a sad state in the 1840s. Some of the smaller windows contained glass, but the large east window did not, and it is clear that the whole of the structure, though still roofed, was broadly open to the elements.

Freemasonry in Scotland

However, there was one group of people already showing a marked interest in Rosslyn Chapel. These men were Freemasons. One of their number, the famed Scottish poet Robert Burns (1759–96), was a fairly regular visitor. A small house that still exists close to the Chapel was in Burns' day an inn, and Burns knew the landlady Meg Wilson so well he even wrote an epigram, which starts 'My blessings on ye, honest wife', about her and the public house.

Burns was not the only Freemason at the time to visit the environs of Rosslyn Chapel, but he may have been partly responsible for 18th-century connections between the Chapel and Freemasonry and could easily have contributed to the renaming of the three important pillars at the eastern end of the Chapel to give them a Freemasonic context. Unfortunately, we know little about the Chapel at this time, and it is difficult to say just how significant it was to rising Freemasonry in the area during the 18th century. We will have much more to say about Rosslyn Chapel and Freemasonry later in this book, but the fact that Rabbie Burns and his fellow Masons showed the reverence they did for the building could be telling.

Freemasonry began early in Scotland, and if some agencies are to be believed, 'very early'. In 1630, Sir William Sinclair of Rosslyn was granted charters from the Masons of Scotland. These confirmed that he was Grand Master of the Scottish Masons. How much this might have had to do with Freemasonry in its current form is open to speculation, but the fact that the connection exists at all is interesting.

Time moved on, and the next we hear about the Chapel is in a royal context. Victoria, Queen of Great Britain from 1837, was married to her German cousin Albert in February 1840. Together, the couple began a love affair not only with each other but also with Scotland, which lasted for the remainder of Victoria's long reign. In September 1842, the young Queen and her consort were visiting Scotland and called in to visit Rosslyn Chapel on the 14th of that month. We know little about the circumstances of her being there, but it is known that she was extremely impressed and suggested that Rosslyn Chapel might well be preserved for the nation.

By 1862, James Alexander was the third Earl of Rosslyn. Perhaps partly in response to the earlier pleas of the monarch, he decided that the time had come to make the Chapel weatherproof and to put it to work as a church. He enlisted the services of architect David Bryce. Over the next three decades the building was gradually improved, and weekly services of an Episcopal nature commenced in 1862. Various repairs were undertaken and more windows glazed. It was in 1869 that the great east window was not only glazed but remodelled, and it was finished with its stained-glass fittings as a memorial to the fourth Earl Francis's sister, the countess of Munster. It was completed by 1871. A baptistry was added to the western end of the building, together with an organ loft in 1881, at the enormous cost of £758.8s.6d. This also led to the first of many coats of obscuring lime wash that eventually covered most of the interior of the Chapel, since the Earl wanted the new baptistry and the Chapel to be the same colour.

In the 1950s, more work on the Chapel was undertaken by the Ministry of Works, which included protecting the carvings with yet another surface coating. This, together with the asphalt laid on the roof, proved to be something of a disaster, though of course it was not realized at the time. In 1995, a conservation report demonstrated that the measures taken in the 1950s had allowed water in the stone to remain there. Chemical salts were eating away at the carvings, and the roof was in a bad state of repair. It was at this time that the Rosslyn Chapel Trust was formed, a body which from that time has run the Chapel, raised money and sought grants to do further repairs.

In 2007, large grants from Historic Scotland and Europe allowed further conservation work to proceed, together with the creation of a new visitor centre. For several years the building was shrouded with a canopy that covered the roof and allowed everything to dry out naturally. Incorporated into the canopy was a walkway that ran around the eastern end of the building above the level of the retrochoir roof. Visitors were allowed access to the walkway, which offered a great view of parts of the exterior of the Chapel that would never normally be seen. It also offered us our first ideas regarding the Rosslyn light box, which we will mention later, and led us to the astronomical discoveries that have been pivotal to our research.

The Story of the Murdered Apprentice

Bearing in mind the magnificence of this structure, together with its definite air of incongruity, perhaps it isn't surprising that the Chapel has always been surrounded by as many myths as true knowledge regarding its history. There is, of course, the connection with Freemasonry. This has become solid enough to ensure that many thousands of Freemasons come throughout the year to visit Rosslyn Chapel. One of the tales they are told relates to the magnificent pillar – the finest of the three that guard the Lady Chapel at the east end of the building. The Freemasonic story suggests that when the building was being created, the master mason was called away on urgent business, leaving his apprentice at the Chapel. While he was absent for a protracted period, the apprentice is said to have had a vision and took it into his head to create the ornate vines that spiral around the pillar from floor to ceiling.

Upon returning, the master mason could scarcely believe his eyes at the incredible beauty of the apprentice's work and, in a fit of rage, envy and jealousy, he took a maul and struck the apprentice on the head, killing him instantly. The whole story is most certainly a fabrication, which is partially drawn from another story that is important to Freemasonry; one that concerns the architect of Solomon's Temple in Jerusalem, a man named Hiram Abif.

High up on the wall of the Chapel is one of four heads that embellish the inner corners of the building. One of these, the closest to the so-called Apprentice Pillar, is meant to be that of a youth – none other than the apprentice himself. It is really nothing of the sort. This face used to be adorned by a beard, but this was brutally hacked off with a hammer, most likely during the late 18th century. What is more, there is a report, over two centuries old, of the landlady from the adjacent inn being seen up a ladder, painting a scar onto the forehead of the stone effigy, the better to have it fit the details of the story. It seems as though the fictional tale of the Apprentice Pillar must have been good for tourist business and was doubtlessly attracting Freemasons already, as it still does today.

Like so much else at Rosslyn Chapel, this particular story has become so deeply engrained into the fabric of the building that it is still related – even by the Chapel guides, who know it to be untrue. But it's a harmless enough fiction, even if the truth of the damaged head and the wrongly named Apprentice Pillar is even more astonishing.

John has lived either in the village of Roslin or very close by for his entire life. His fascination for the Chapel has been with him from childhood, and since he grew to become a professional film cameraman, he has been able to put together probably the greatest number of still and moving images of the place ever assembled, as well as spending years learning everything he could about the true history of the Chapel.

Alan was introduced to the Chapel around 15 years ago and met John at that time. In addition to a close friendship, the association has been led by a common desire to dig ever deeper into the history of Rosslyn Chapel, to dispel the myths and to replace them with observable and provable truths.

We have delved into every corner of Rosslyn Chapel, turned up every document we could and looked at the structure in the light of talents and research backgrounds that had not been applied to it before. Nevertheless, we listened carefully to the folk tales because we both recognize that these can either carry, or point to, something genuinely important, which indeed has turned out to be the case.

In 2006, we published our first book on the Chapel, entitled *Rosslyn Revealed*.[2] Since then we have continued to research and have plugged away at a number of leads that had not been available previously. We have had to modify a few of our original thoughts as a result, and we have come to some fairly radical conclusions that would have been impossible back then.

It has to be admitted that some very unlikely and even some quite silly suggestions have been made about Rosslyn Chapel and its history. What we never expected, either in our initial research or more recently, was how much more strange, intriguing and astonishing the truth would turn out to be.

CHAPTER TWO

In Search of a Saint

I n the early days of our common research we were anxious to look at evidence regarding Rosslyn Chapel that had not been pawed over for decades already. It seemed to us that we had a better chance of discovering more about this mysterious place if we started from scratch, rather than relying on what were sometimes suspect stories. Many of these were based on hearsay and tales that may well have become distorted with the passing of time and constant retelling.

We went right back to the beginning and asked ourselves, what do we know for sure about Rosslyn Chapel? As a result we created a sizeable list, high upon which was the fact that the Chapel had been dedicated to St Matthew. Since nothing regarding the dedication had been commented upon in any way by other researchers, we thought it was worth discovering more. As is so often the case in historical research, it could easily have proved to be a dead end, but in this case it turned out to be critically important.

The dedication of any given church to a specific saint was not, and probably still isn't, a haphazard business. It can come about for a host of different reasons. For example, in large medieval cities, people who were employed in the same business often lived in tight communities. Goldsmiths, silversmiths, coopers, cobblers and so many other trades and professions usually occupied the same streets as everyone else doing the same job, and most individuals lived over the shop. Their children would often intermarry and because they did, there was less chance that the secrets or 'mysteries', as they were called, of any particular occupation would pass to outsiders. Thus, whole communities sprang up that had much in common – even when it came to their place of worship.

If a church in a busy medieval city such as Edinburgh or York was created in the butcher's district, it would most likely be dedicated to St Anthony. This is because in medieval Christianity there was a specific saint for just about everything – including saints who were seen as being responsive to specific trades or professions. For the same reasons a new parish church built in the goldsmith's district may well be dedicated to St Eligius, whilst coopers and barrel makers would most probably have dedicated their local church to St Nicholas.

Of course in the case of a small community, such a state of affairs would not apply. Inhabitants of the average village did not have a profession in common – there would be all manner of workers present in the district, so it often came down to the preference of whoever *owned* the village, in other words the local squire. In England, and also to a lesser degree in Scotland, many of the biggest landowners in medieval times were Norman French in origin. Their families may well have had a preferred saint for centuries and he or she would undoubtedly have been the dedicated saint when a new church was built.

Sometimes the dedication would be to a very local saint – someone from the area who, back in the mists of time, had risen to sainthood in the early Church. At other times the presence of a church would record a specific event. For example, when the Vikings began to pillage the northeast of England in AD 875, they threatened the monastic settlement at Lindisfarne, where the bones of a revered Scottish saint by the name of Cuthbert were kept. The monks at the monastery fled with the bones, on a protracted journey of seven years. During this time Cuthbert's bones found sanctuary in all manner of places before eventually ending up near Durham. It is possible even today to trace where the monks stopped for any length of time by the fact that such communities still have a parish church dedicated to St Cuthbert.

✝ · ✝ · ✝

All of this is very interesting, but what does it tell us about the dedication of Rosslyn Chapel to St Matthew? It is clear that St Matthew is not a local saint. He is not even the patron saint of the Sinclair family – that place is held by St Catherine. Also, in our estimation this dedication had nothing to do with a saint historically associated with the family who built the chapel. The builder was William Sinclair, whose family name had originally been St Clair, which is a saint's name in itself. St Clair is a French version of the Latin name 'Clarus', after whom the Sinclairs, originally a Norman French family, were named.

If the Scottish Sinclair lords had chosen to use a church dedication that had been important to their family's past, it would surely have been St Clarus? So, if the dedication had nothing to do with a trade or profession, if the saint was not of a local origin and if there was no family link, could the dedication have had been associated in some way with one of the attributes of St Matthew? If we were going to understand why William Sinclair chose to build a St Matthew's church on his land, and especially one so impressive, we would need to know more about the saint in question.

The Importance of St Matthew

As it turned out, St Matthew is one of the better-known saints of the Christian Church. This is because, according to Church tradition, Matthew was one of the original disciples of Jesus, as well as being a writer of one of the four Gospels of the New Testament of the Bible. Representations of St Matthew always show him with a book, often with an angel and a book, and also sometimes with a bag of money and a book. The book is said to be representative of the Gospel St Matthew wrote but he is not known as the patron saint of writers. On the grounds that he was a tax collector before he became a disciple of Jesus, St Matthew is known as being the patron saint of account-ants, bankers, money managers, civil servants, guards, security guards and, of course, tax collectors.

Not a great deal is known for sure about the real St Matthew. This is not too surprising because we don't know very much about any of the primary characters involved in the ministry of Jesus. What the New Testament tells us is that Matthew was collecting taxes at a booth in the street when Jesus saw and called him. In Palestine during the 1st century, any person of Jewish origin who turned to tax collecting would have been a social pariah. Taxes were collected for and on behalf of the Romans, who had conquered the region and were themselves generally disliked, if not despised. A modern interpretation of the calling of such an individual to be a disciple would be that Jesus carried a message for *all* people, not merely the virtuous. After all, he also associated with prostitutes and lepers. So St Matthew, a Jew from the tribe of Levi, became a follower of Christ.

What Jesus would certainly have found in Matthew was an intelligent and even literate person in terms of education and social class. Matthew would have certainly been a cut above the humble fishermen who were also amongst the first followers of Jesus, according to the New Testament of the Bible.

Of the four Gospels of the New Testament, that of St Matthew is sequentially the first. Probably for this reason it was always considered that it was also the first to be written. Modern researchers are less sure about this, with many preferring to plump for Mark as the oldest of the Gospels. In truth, the whole situation is extremely complicated, with some experts even suggesting that parts of the existing Gospels were taken from a fifth, now unknown gospel. Much of the confusion springs from the fact that Christianity developed in generally troubled times. Early Christians were not universally popular, to the point that they were persecuted, especially so by the Roman authorities. At the same time, these first Christians were often hated by orthodox Jews. They represented an underground sect, and although the popularity of the cult spread quite quickly, it wasn't until the reign of the Roman Emperor Constantine, in the 4th century, that Christians were allowed to worship freely everywhere. Eventually Constantine went one stage further, when at the Council of Nicaea in AD 325 Christianity was effectively made the state religion of the Roman Empire.

The Development of the Christian Church

Prior to this great gathering, Christianity had developed along many different lines. The very first Church had been wholly Jewish in nature, and even when it began to spread amongst non-Jewish people, it often took on radically different forms and was affected by other beliefs and traditions in specific areas. By the time Constantine chose to adopt Christianity himself, he took on a hotchpotch of differing traditions, views and opinions, many of which had been developing in their own way for a couple of centuries or more. However, if Christianity was going to *serve* the Roman Empire in the way Constantine required, it was obvious that it would have to be standardized – otherwise it could not be state-controlled. As a result, following the Council of Nicaea, the representatives of opposing Christian sects were expected to bury their differences and to create something standard and recognizable. Once a party line had been established, everyone was expected to follow it – to the point that certain Christians once again suffered persecution if they failed to adopt the Emperor's sanctioned beliefs and practices.

We could easily write an entire book itemizing all the different thoughts regarding the date and order in which the Gospels were written, but the truth is, despite strident arguments, especially during the last two centuries, nobody really knows. It is clear that *all* the Gospels have been subject to significant modification, much of which took place around the time of the Council of Nicaea or immediately after. It also seems certain that parts of some of the Gospels were later added to others, and doubtless information in any of them that did not square with what was required by the State Church was eradicated. The situation is so complicated that although it offers scholars lifetimes of diligent study and comment, it is unlikely that, 2,000 years later, we will ever get to the truth of who the Gospel writers really were, or understand what their narratives originally looked like.

At the time Constantine came to power, in AD 306, the Roman Empire was literally falling to pieces. Some areas were fighting for autonomy against the Empire, whilst others were being invaded by barbarians from outside. The adoption of a common religion was just one of the strategies Constantine thought up to try and weld the desperate parts of his Empire back together. The Romans had never been particularly forthright about religion. On the contrary, successive Emperors didn't much care what anyone believed, just as long as that faith did not affect the running of the Empire. Throughout the huge geographical area in question there were hundreds of different beliefs and cults. It followed that any 'one' religion that could be adopted by all those under the Roman yoke would have to be flexible enough to cope with pre-existing beliefs.

At the start of Constantine's reign, Christianity was not necessarily the only contender for the Emperor's new way forward. Before conversion, Constantine himself had followed the mystery religion of Mithras. Like Christianity, Mithraism had spread extensively throughout the Empire, mainly because it was the preferred religion of Roman soldiers. For Christianity to succeed, it would have to entice other believers, and especially the followers of Mithras, to come on board. To this end, Christianity had to be somewhat altered, and that sometimes meant making changes to the very books that stood at the heart of the faith – the Gospels.

As just one example, the whole part of the Christian story dealing with the nativity of Jesus was undoubtedly added to some of the Gospels at a later date. This has to be the case because incidents associated with the birth of Jesus, and even some related to his death, are *identical* to aspects of Mithraism. Since the cult of Mithras was older than Christianity, it stands to reason that incidents such as the Virgin birth, and the death and resurrection of Christianity's leading figure, were added later, so that followers of Mithras could more easily adopt Christianity. If some readers doubt this assessment, they should be aware that there came a time (date unknown) when the Christian Church actually started to preach that the similarities between Christianity and Mithraism had been placed into Mithraism at an earlier time by the Devil himself, as a deliberate ploy to lead later Christians astray. To our ears this sounds absurd, but it most certainly happened.

Of the fact that Jesus had a disciple named Matthew, there is little doubt. At the same time it cannot be denied that one of the four Gospels carries the name of Matthew. Whether or not the two characters are one and the same is unknown, but perhaps the important fact is that early Christianity believed they were. St Matthew is mentioned very little in the Bible, and all of the tales associated with his life after Jesus' death, apart from a couple of fragmentary references in the Gospels, come from stories that were written much later. They are part of the traditions of the early Church Fathers, which represent whole sequences of books, some of which are genuinely very old, and others that are of much more recent origin.

One of the most interesting facts about St Matthew is just how important his particular Gospel was to certain groups of early Christians who would end up being persecuted by the Church itself. We know about these groups, not through their own words, which have been destroyed wherever they existed, but from the mouths of those within the Church who disapproved and sought to exterminate them.

The Testimony of Irenaeus

One such commentator, whose writings we came to look at closely, was a man by the name of Irenaeus, an early Church Father in Christian history. We don't know when he was born, but his death is said to have occurred in AD 202. Irenaeus was born in Ephesus, but he ultimately became a priest and eventually the Bishop of Lyon, in France. Irenaeus was born into interesting times; Christianity was fragmented, its believers were often persecuted and in some places the cult was still illegal. Irenaeus was one of those who obviously realized that Christianity would never survive and flourish unless all its branches could be persuaded to follow the same teaching and the same traditions. To that end he became an outspoken critic of those he considered heretical to the faith as he saw it.

In his writings, Irenaeus had a great deal to say about a large number of sects of Christianity of which he did not approve. He accused some of these of following false teachings. Irenaeus was a Pauline Christian. This means he followed the teachings of St Paul, an early convert to Christianity, but not one of Jesus' disciples. St Paul, although Jewish himself, introduced Christianity to Gentiles; he does not appear to have got on well with, or been approved of, by the Jerusalem Church, which of course was the original branch of the faith and which, in the years immediately after Jesus' death, was being inspired by Jesus' direct followers.

By the time Irenaeus was writing his criticisms, the St Paul version of Christianity had gained ground. This was especially true in Rome, partly because St Paul had eventually been taken to Rome and was executed there. Meanwhile, back in Palestine and the surrounding areas, groups of Christians that owed nothing to St Paul but everything to the Jerusalem Church, still had their own followings. In this confused atmosphere, Christianity certainly had not come of age and which group would predominate was still by no means certain. Irenaeus was extremely vitriolic about groups he considered to be heretical, and no group came in for greater criticism than the Ebionites.

We learn from Irenaeus that the Ebionites, still a large group in his time and who were mainly located in the eastern part of the Roman Empire, did not believe in the Virgin birth, and although they accepted the teachings of Jesus, they did not worship him as the Messiah or hold to the notion that he was the one and only Son of God. What turned out to be of particular interest to us was the fact that Irenaeus accused the Ebionites of showing great reverence to the Gospel of Matthew, to the exclusion of all other gospels. However, also according to Irenaeus, the version of Matthew revered by the Ebionites was 'incomplete'. We can probably take this to mean that the story of the Nativity and most likely the tales of Jesus' resurrection were not included. The Ebionites, like other groups at the time, also showed a particular reverence for John the Baptist.

This seems to imply that an earlier version of St Matthew's Gospel than the one used by the Romans, Pauline Christians *did* exist. It was almost certainly written in Aramaic and not

Greek and was in circulation in and around Palestine, as late as the 3rd century AD. This might explain why modern researchers consider that parts of St Matthew's Gospel owed something to that of St Mark because sizeable chunks had been added to Matthew's original gospel from other sources – most likely the Gospel of St Mark. In other words, the gospel of St Matthew revered by the Ebionites was an original, Aramaic gospel that the Pauline Christians had not adulterated.

This seems to make the original St Matthew a powerful force in the form of Christianity that proliferated in and around Palestine, though by the time of the Emperor Constantine, groups like the Ebionites became marginalized. They were subsequently destroyed or driven underground. And of course, by this period, St Matthew's gospel had been 'doctored' so that it told the same story as all the other Gospels. It has to be admitted that there is a fair degree of speculation involved here. The Roman, Pauline Christians became ruthless in their attacks on any different forms of Christianity and certainly destroyed any written material that did not conform to their own beliefs and explanations. They wanted the *form* of Christianity that they and the Emperor had synthesized – and no other sort.

What all this information taught us, in our initial investigations, was that Matthew had been associated from a very early date with a form of Christianity that was quite distinct from the Roman Catholicism that eventually developed in the West. None of this really meant much to us at the time, but in the following months the situation came much more into focus.

✛ · ✛ · ✛

In the meantime we concentrated on the stories about St Matthew that had developed in the years before and after Constantine formalized the faith in the West. Even then there wasn't a great deal. There tended to be two schools of thought regarding St Matthew. One series of stories suggested he had been martyred, whilst other commentators said he had *not*.

Learning more about St Matthew

According to *The International Standard Bible Encyclopaedia*, Matthew preached in Judaea for 15 years after Jesus' death, after which he travelled to Ethiopia, Macedonia, Persia and Parthia. Matthew's connection with Ethiopia is also attested in Islamic writings of a very early period.

Details of St Matthew's life are not as common as those of his contemporary St Paul, and not all commentators these days believe what was once held as correct, namely that Matthew's was the original gospel and had been known as the Gospel of the Hebrews. It is, however, generally held that Matthew was the most intellectual of the original disciples, and it seems to make sense that if any amongst the twelve had committed the story of Jesus and his teaching to Aramaic, Hebrew and possibly even Greek, it would have been Matthew, if only because of his station in life. Meanwhile, any information about the real St Matthew tends to be obscured by stories that developed at an unknown, but clearly very early, period.

The most comprehensive of these is to be found in a work called the *Ante-Nicene Fathers*: Volume 8. It comes from what is known as the Apocrypha – biblical writings of generally unknown origin that are definitely early in date, but which did not appear in the Hebrew canon. Within the Apocrypha is to be found a detailed account of the events leading up to the death of St Matthew in an otherwise unidentified city by the name of Myrna – unidentified unless it is synonymous with Smyrna, in which case it becomes Izmir in modern Turkey. The whole of this account can be found in the Appendix. Briefly, we are told that St Matthew travelled to the city called Myrna in order to visit a church that he and a fellow disciple, St Andrew, had founded sometime earlier.

Myrna was clearly a sinful place and is referred to in the narrative as the 'City of the Man eaters'. Prior to arriving at Myrna, Matthew was approached by a small child who, unbeknown to Matthew, was actually Jesus. The child gave him a staff and instructed him to go to Myrna and to plant the staff into the ground outside the church. He was informed that upon doing so, a great and wonderful tree would grow from the staff. The tree would have rivers at its base, where mystic creatures swam, and a huge canopy, with every branch carrying a different form of fruit, 12 in all, 1 for every month of the year. There was said to be a source of sweetness from above. Honey would drop down from the branches of the tree, which would offer food and shade against the heat for the citizens of Myrna.

Matthew did as he was bid, and everything came to pass as the child had told him. There are different versions of what followed, but most of these suggest that, despite this miracle, Matthew was martyred in Myrna on the orders of its wicked king. In some versions of the story it is suggested that he was beheaded, which is why an axe is sometimes depicted with the saint.

The stories, and fragments of stories, did not give us much to go on, until we stopped to think about the situation subsequently. When we did, we realized almost immediately that in terms of its ornamentation, Rosslyn Chapel did indeed owe a great deal to St Matthew, and for a very important reason.

The Importance of the Ornate Pillar

Everyone who has visited Rosslyn, and even many people who have studied it through photographs, immediately becomes familiar with the most northerly of the three ornate pillars that stand in front of the Lady Chapel at the east end. Incorrectly referred to as the Apprentice Pillar (*see* Chapter One) it is a tour de force of the stone carvers' art. It is a fluted pillar, but circling and spiralling around it is a deep foliate design, the leaves of which resemble those of a vine – four vines, to be precise, with eight threads forming the vines that issue from the mouths of the dragons or creatures that swim at the base of the column.

We had observed, way back at the start of our research, that all the foliate and naturalistic designs carved in Rosslyn Chapel ultimately emanate from the bottom of this pillar. There is none that develops from other places low down on the Chapel's inner walls. Most likely, each of the four vines represents a season and is tied to the pillar with the twin thread of life, each thread issuing from the mouths of the eight dragons or Yggdrasil (the Nordic Tree of Life), which is created by the joining of the two skeins holding the vines to the pillar. The truth of this pillar, which we now dare to call St Matthew's Pillar, seems to have been totally lost to anyone associated with the Chapel, and indeed it may never have been made generally known, but of what it represents there can now be no doubt whatsoever. St Matthew's pillar is a representation of the trunk of the tree created by Matthew at Myrna from the staff of life given to him for the purpose, by the Christ child. In a representational sense and in line with a number of belief patterns it represents the tree that links earthly things to heaven and is sometimes referred to as 'the staff of life'.

How do we know this must be the case? In fact, it is obvious for many reasons, some of which make an identification of the pillar with the Myrna tree unequivocal. Look at these words from the Apocrypha that Matthew speaks about the tree:

> … and it shall be a sign to your generations, and it shall become a tree, great and lofty and flourishing, and its fruit beautiful to the view and good to the sight; and the fragrance of perfumes shall come forth from it, and there shall be a vine twining round it, full of clusters;

The vine twining round the tree is mentioned not one but three times in the story, and its description closely approximates what we see in the Chapel. We are told in the story that the tree had many branches, and that from each branch a different form of fruit grew that would feed the people of Myrna. This is exactly what we find carved onto the Chapel walls. Branches and tendrils ultimately emanate from the top of St Matthew's pillar upon which many different forms of fruit can be seen. These represent none other than the extensive foliate and nature designs for which Rosslyn Chapel is ultimately so famous, the presence of which have puzzled casual visitors and experts alike.

If anyone is still doubtful that this magnificent pillar is meant to represent St Matthew's tree in Myrna, the case becomes proved when we look at another part of the story. Just after the last quote come the next words of the sentence:

> and there shall be a vine twining round it, full of
> clusters; and from the top of it honey coming down,

Alan well remembers all those years ago when John first took him on an extensive tour of the Chapel. At that time, the roof canopy and visitor walkway were in place. As we walked up the slope on the north side, towards the east end of the Chapel, John pointed to one of the impressive pinnacles that stand high above the roof of the Lady Chapel. "Have you noticed all the bees flying round here?" he asked. "That's because this pinnacle is also a beehive."

Alan asked if the bees had got into the pinnacle by accident. Nobody was absolutely sure, although it had been reported since time out of mind that the bees made a nest there each summer. It was also said by older parishioners that, at the height of the summer, honey from the pinnacle hive found its way from the roof of the Lady Chapel and dripped down onto Matthew's altar below, we believe as a form of libation.

It wasn't until the final stages of the renovations of the Chapel in 2011 that the full truth of the story was known. At that time the pyramidal top was removed from the pinnacle, showing the evidence of many successive hives of wild bees inside. It was later discovered that many of the finials had beehives, but most had been filled with stones during the Victorian restorations. It would have been wonderful to hear the sound in the chapel if all the bees from all the finial hives were buzzing at the same time.

It was also discovered that there was a hole through one of the ceiling bosses above the altar, directly below the pinnacle. This had been deliberately created and was the route the wild honey took before it dripped down onto Matthew's altar below; very obviously '*the source of sweetness from above*'.

Like the vine around the trunk of Matthew's tree, the honey was mentioned several times in the Apocryphal text called 'Acts and Martyrdom of St Matthew', and each time there is the same specific reference to the honey dripping down from the tree.

We suggest that there can no longer be any doubt about the truth underpinning much of the wonderful stone carving on the interior of the Chapel, and especially that at the east end and on the south wall. When it was new, it was also painted in vivid colours, offering an almost three-dimensional representation of the tree that Matthew created from the staff in Myrna. Through the ingenuity and artifice of those who planned the Chapel, it had even been possible to replicate the honey mentioned in the story, dripping down from the branches of the tree.

Bearing all this in mind, we both hope that the hard-working guides at Rosslyn Chapel will take this information on board. Of course we expect them to relate the story of the Apprentice Pillar; it's certainly nonsense, but we appreciate that it is *interesting* nonsense. However, this ought to be offset by a description of the *truth* of the matter, which is so much more compelling and fully backed by all the evidence that is right in front of the eyes of anyone visiting the Chapel. Truth is, indeed, often stranger and more wonderful than fiction.

CHAPTER THREE

The Bones
of the Holy

A t the time we were putting the finishing touches to our first book written together, *Rosslyn Revealed*, we had just come across a piece of information that nobody had noticed before, and which associated Rosslyn Chapel with an important individual by the name of Sir Gilbert Hayee.

Sir Gilbert Haye was a member of a prominent Scottish family – the Hays of Errol. He was born around 1403, and what we went on to learn about him proved that he was obviously well educated. His grandfather had been a personal friend of King Robert the Bruce and had fought alongside him through many struggles against the English. In recognition of his tireless service and his loyalty, Gilbert's grandfather, also Sir Gilbert, was given the hereditary title of Lord High Constable of Scotland.

We knew that the Sir Gilbert Haye, who interested us, had been educated at St Andrew's University in Scotland and left in 1419 to continue a doctorate in Paris in 1420. Absolute details of his life are sketchy, but of his ultimate achievements there can be no doubt. Gilbert Haye went on to become a poet, a writer, a translator, a high-ranking librarian and the chamberlain to the French King in 1433.

It seems Sir Gilbert was an all-round genius. He was certainly at Reims in France in July 1430, at the coronation of Charles VII of France, and was undoubtedly high in the estimation of Charles at that time because he was knighted. Later, he would become, as the language of the day put it, 'chaumerlayn umquhyle to the maist worthy King Charles of France'. In fact, he was much more because he became King Charles's librarian. This was at a time when only really wealthy people and the Church could afford to have books of any sort, and we know that Charles VII was an avid collector of both religious and secular works. Printing had not yet been invented, so the whole of Charles's extensive library would have represented hand-written, and usually sumptuously adorned, volumes.

It is also certain that Gilbert Haye travelled a great deal during his lifetime, though where his journeys took him is impossible to say. He was on good terms with other rulers, and especially René of Anjou, Count of Guise, Duke of Lorraine and ultimately King of Naples. René thrived on education and had a peerless library of his own. Gilbert Haye's relationship to René of Anjou would eventually become important to our whole story.

By 1456, Sir Gilbert Haye was back in his native Scotland. Perhaps he had retired from his service to the French king by this time because if we assume he was born around 1403, he would have been 53 when he returned to Scotland – a not inconsiderable age for the period. So, did Sir Gilbert decide to go to Edinburgh, to become a member of the royal circle there? In fact he did not; rather, he chose to become tutor to the children of Sir William Sinclair at his home in Rosslyn.

We consider Sir Gilbert Haye's importance to the Sinclair family, and especially to Rosslyn Chapel, to be second to none, and it is quite possible that his appointment as tutor to William Sinclair's household was a convenient cover for what turned out to be a much more important job. All of this should become clear presently, but what interested us most about Sir Gilbert at this particular moment related to a scrap of information that John had discovered, written in Gilbert's own hand, in the margin of a famous Scottish Book called the *Scotichronicon* which Gilbert had been editing for his St Andrews contemporary, Walter Bower. The short extract made it plain that Sir Gilbert Haye had, at some time, visited a thriving abbey in Brittany. There he had been shown what was purported to be the skull of St Matthew.

An Abbey in Brittany

The abbey in question was known as the abbey Saint-Mathieu de Fine-Terre. Its ruins can still be seen overlooking the sea at the appropriately named Pointe St-Mathieu, not far from the city of Brest. The abbey was a Benedictine foundation and was begun in the 11th century. It soon became rich and prosperous, mainly because of the supposed presence there of St Matthew's skull. How the skull came to be in such a strange and turbulent place is the subject of three of four local stories. The most complete of these relates that, as early as the 9th century, Breton traders had come across the relics of St Matthew in the East and had brought them home to Brittany. The same legend asserts that in the 10th century the relics of St Matthew (not just the skull) were taken by the Normans from Brittany to Naples in Italy, where it is suggested they lie in the Cathedral of Salerno. If this story was true in its entirety, it is hard to see how the abbey in Brittany flourished over the next 400 years. It became a major site of pilgrimage and was endowed with money from both the visitors and from the English and the dukes of Brittany.

This windswept spot has been the scene of numerous battles. For centuries, Brittany considered itself to be quite separate from the Kingdom of France, and the dukes of Brittany often sided with the English. As a result of constant fighting between the Breton-supported English and the French, the abbey and the little port close by changed hands time and again. The abbey buildings were ravaged and rebuilt on several occasions. In one such skirmish, in 1296, the relics of St Matthew were taken from the abbey by the English Earl of Leicester, but were apparently quickly returned. All the while, and despite the supposed presence of the relics in far-off Italy, the abbey St-Mathieu flourished and grew larger. In other words, in the estimation of the thousands of pilgrims who found their way to this coastal settlement, at least part of St Matthew was definitely housed there.

The Importance of Relics

Before we go any further with the story of St Matthew's skull, it is necessary to point out just how important and valuable such a supposed item would have been to those who held it. Almost since the dawn of humanity it seems that people have wanted to keep and to revere objects, or even parts of the bodies, belonging to those who had the reputation of being particularly magical or holy. The gathering and keeping of relics is far older than Christianity – for example, it flourishes in Buddhism and numerous other beliefs; indeed in Bon Po Buddhism, one of the oldest forms of Tibetan Buddhism, lamas have rosaries made up of small pieces of skull from deceased lamas. It is probably not surprising then that early in the history of the Christian Church, relics became important, most likely because at a time when Christianity was often under threat, relics were a tangible link between beleaguered Christians and those who began the religion.

By the end of the first millennium the possession of saints' relics by specific cathedrals and abbeys was starting to become big business. Pilgrims would travel for weeks or months to view such relics or simply to be in their presence. Under the circumstances, and bearing in mind that many of the most precious relics dated back to a time when nothing was committed to paper and legends were as important as the truth, the provenance of any given relic was dubious to say the least. Just as one example, it is often stated that if all the supposed pieces of the true Cross, on which Jesus was crucified, were brought together from their various homes across the globe, it would be possible to create a sizeable ship from them, maybe even an ark. There can be no doubt that many relics were mistakenly attributed or were downright forgeries.

To a generally gullible public, at least until the 16th century, this does not seem to have mattered one jot; the Church vouched for specific relics and that was enough. What was more, numerous miracles attached themselves to relics and the places where they were kept, which only served to convince pilgrims that they were genuine. At the end of the day, it probably did not matter at all whether a relic had anything to do with the saint in question. What mattered, both materially and perhaps even spiritually, was the fact that the majority of people *believed* they were genuine, so it was the investment of belief in the piece that gave the relic its hallowed spirituality.

Genuine or not, relics were extremely important, and any cathedral or abbey that wanted to prosper and flourish simply had to have them. Relics brought pilgrims and pilgrims brought money – in all forms. One only has to look at the power and wealth of establishments such as Canterbury Cathedral in England to see just what relics meant. In the case of Canterbury, where the relics of the martyred St Thomas Becket were housed, there was no doubt about their authenticity. However, St Thomas Becket had not died until 1170, whereas St Matthew had personally known and been called by Jesus himself. Relics relating to the disciples were the most prized of all – because they represented the biggest pull as far as believers were concerned.

✠ · ✠ · ✠

We are both well aware that the chance of the bones, and especially the skull of St Matthew – about whom we know almost nothing apart from a few scant mentions in the Gospels – having survived the turbulent, anti-Christian period in which he lived and died, is negligible. However, since even an intelligent man such as Sir Gilbert Haye clearly believed that the relics at abbey St-Mathieu in Brittany were genuine, our own considerations, here in the 21st century, mean nothing.

The strange thing about the skull of St Matthew in its abbey home in Brittany is that it suddenly and mysteriously disappeared from the annals of history at some time more or less immediately after Sir Gilbert Haye had reported seeing it there. In a way, it is probably just as well, because by the third quarter of the 1400s, control of Brittany fell to the French Crown. This was something the English could not stomach. During this period the so-called Hundred Years' War was being fought between England and France. As late as 1429, the whole of Brittany was controlled by the English, who were only driven out by the middle of the century.

In other words, Brittany was in a constant state of ferment, and the Pointe de St-Mathieu, sticking out into the ocean, was always in danger of being attacked from the sea. We can find no reference to the presence of St Matthew's skull in Brittany after the mid 1400s. Had it remained there it would almost certainly have been destroyed in 1558, when a large English fleet ravaged Brest and much of the coastline of Brittany, including the settlement of St-Mathieu. Back in 1529, Henry VIII of England had broken his religious affiliation to Rome. This had been followed by a wholesale dissolution of the monastic houses and other religious foundations in England. Concurrently, Henry gave orders that saints' relics were to be destroyed. As a result, if St Matthew's skull had been in the abbey St-Mathieu in 1558, it would undoubtedly have been lost.

Reliquaries

We now come to the fascinating subject of reliquaries. It stands to reason that if the bodily relics or items that once belonged to a saint are considered precious and holy, they would deserve to be kept in a safe and secure casket of some sort. This is exactly what happened, and as the centuries progressed, more and more time and money was spent on these receptacles, which are known collectively as reliquaries.

Reliquaries came in all shapes and sizes. If, for example, the supposed leg of a saint was revered in a particular place, it would often be kept in a reliquary that represented the shape of a human leg. These were far from being plain and simple affairs. On the contrary, they were often made of gold and silver and were sometimes encrusted with precious stones. This is one of the reasons why England's King Henry VIII was so keen to destroy the cult of relics in the 16th century. To him, and his Protestant-leaning courtiers, the reliquaries were worth far more than the bones, and as a result, they usually ended up being melted down for bullion, with the gems and highly enamelled pieces used in jewellery.

Not all reliquaries were shaped like parts of a human body. The earliest examples were just caskets, but right from the start there was a tendency to give them an architectural form. In some cases they were meant to represent miniature versions of the churches and chapels where they were housed, or they might have an architectural form in some way related to the life or circumstances of the saint.

Reliquaries gradually became bigger, more ornate and more precious, with the pinnacle of their production and the finest examples being in the 14th century. The more important the saint, the greater the time and money spent on the reliquary, with the result that in at least one example the reliquary was no longer a casket at all – it was an entire building.

For many centuries, the crown of thorns worn by Jesus prior to his crucifixion had supposedly survived, and was said to have been kept, at least from the 5th century onwards, in the basilica on Mount Zion in Jerusalem. As the region became threatened by Islam, the relic was moved progressively until it ended up in Constantinople (present-day Istanbul). In 1238, the ruler of the region was a Latin Emperor named Baldwin. He found himself in serious financial difficulties and so he pawned the Crown of Thorns to Venetian bankers. The relic remained with the bankers until Louis IX (later St Louis) provided the money to release them and brought them to France. They arrived in Paris on 9 August 1239 and were eventually housed in a structure specifically created for them. It was not a church, since it had none of the usual furnishings, but rather it was a giant reliquary, with large and sumptuous stained-glass windows telling the story of Christ and the Crown of Thorns itself. This building still stands and is open to the public. It no longer holds the Crown of Thorns, which is kept at Notre Dame Cathedral, so it is just a large, empty and very beautiful box, known as Sainte-Chapelle.

Nobody is in any doubt. When Sainte-Chapelle was built in the centre of Paris, it was deliberately designed to be a giant reliquary – not just for the Crown of Thorns but for numerous other relics in King Louis's collection. It has been described as a 'reliquary turned inside out' because the exquisite workmanship is represented by the stained glass, carvings and panels within the building, whereas in the case of most reliquaries the embellishment is on the outside. But a reliquary it is nevertheless, and since it was built to serve no other purpose, it is probably the largest reliquary in the world. It might be argued that some cathedrals were built to house the relics of saints, but they served, and serve, numerous other purposes, which Sainte-Chapelle did not. Some cathedrals and churches may *contain* reliquaries, but they cannot be said to *be* reliquaries, which Sainte-Chapelle can.

A Letter from Mary of Guise

Mindful of this, we were forced to think about the disappearance of the supposed skull of St Matthew from Brittany, the design of Rosslyn Chapel and a curious letter that was sent by Mary of Guise to Sir William Sinclair in 1546, by which time Rosslyn Chapel was approaching 100 years since its foundation. The Sir William Sinclair in question was, of course, a direct descendent of the William Sinclair, who had built the Chapel. That he was on good terms with Mary of Guise is not surprising, but the letter she wrote to him definitely is.

Mary of Guise was the second wife of King James V of Scotland and the mother of his only surviving child, who would come to be known by history as Mary, Queen of Scots. By the time Mary of Guise wrote her letter to Sir William Sinclair in 1546, her husband, King James, had been dead for four years, which meant she was the dowager queen of Scotland and that her daughter was the new infant queen of the country. All of this made Mary of Guise a powerful individual and makes the tenor of her letter to William Sinclair that much more puzzling.

A passage of the letter in question reads:

> We bind and oblige us to the said Sir William, and
> shall be a loyal and true mistress to him. His counsel

and secret shown to us we shall keep secret, and in
all matters give to him the best and truest counsel
we can, as we shall be required thereto.

The wording of the letter is strange indeed. True, William
Sinclair was a powerful aristocrat and an important ally to the
Scottish throne, but Mary of Guise was a queen, as well as being
the mother of the reigning monarch. It is therefore very odd
that she should refer to herself as Sir William's *loyal and true
mistress*. Obviously, the term mistress did not carry its modern
connotation, but it still suggests a position of humility that
sounds unusual in the case of a monarch talking to a subject.

This letter has become very important to researchers trying
to discover the supposed 'treasure' of Rosslyn Chapel because
it definitely indicates that Mary of Guise had, during her visit
to Rosslyn Castle and Chapel, seen or heard something that
she deemed to be extremely significant. We asked ourselves
whether or not the object in question could possibly have been
the skull of St Matthew that Sir Gilbert Haye had reported
visiting in Brittany?

Our reasoning stemmed from a number of different factors,
but high on the list was our earlier discovery that so many of
the carvings on the interior of Rosslyn Chapel related directly
to St Matthew, and particularly to the only truly intact story
about his life – namely his visit to the city of Myrna and the
miracle he performed there.

Once this realization had been made, we began to look at
the Chapel and its ornamentation in a slightly different way.
It cannot be denied that Rosslyn Chapel is a strange building.
It is small and squat, and, particularly when seen from the air,

it bears a striking similarity to a number of 13th- and 14th-century reliquaries that have managed to survive to the present day, especially in France and Belgium.

In particular, it is incredibly like the reliquary of St Taurin, who was venerated in Evreux, Normandy, France. A picture of St Taurin's reliquary, which was made in 1247 can be seen in the colour section of the book. The general shape of this reliquary and its architectural details are uncannily like Rosslyn Chapel. Where it differs significantly is that, like most reliquaries, it is heavily adorned on the outside, offering images from the supposed life and mission of St Taurin. Meanwhile, Rosslyn Chapel carries its information regarding St Matthew (for whom the Chapel was dedicated) on the inside, as is the case with Sainte-Chapelle in Paris.

Our observations regarding the true significance of the story of St Matthew at Myrna, which had been lost from history prior to our own investigations, showed that a large percentage of the sumptuous carving in Rosslyn Chapel, and especially at the eastern end, was totally dedicated to this one event. The branches and tendrils of the mythical tree of Myrna spread out around the Chapel, with their many forms of leaves and fruits. High above, the vault of the ceiling, with its many stars, mimics the vault of the sky itself, increasing the feeling that the designers of the Chapel wished those viewing the spectacle to imagine themselves out of doors. Thus, it becomes obvious that, no matter what else one is *supposed* to take from the interior carvings of Rosslyn Chapel, the story of St Matthew is paramount.

This state of affairs is very unusual in terms of normal church architecture and decoration. Clearly, in almost any medieval church one would expect to find references to the saint for whom the church was dedicated, but in the case of Rosslyn Chapel this is carried to what might seem to be an absurd extreme – unless, of course, Rosslyn Chapel was quite deliberately created to not only offer reverence to St Matthew – but also a form of sanctuary.

Putting aside for now *why* Sir William Sinclair might have wanted to bring an important relic of St Matthew to Scotland and there create a sumptuous and huge reliquary to house it, we first had to ask ourselves whether such a thing was likely or possible. After examining the facts we came to the conclusion that the proposal was not far-fetched at all, and for a number of reasons.

Proximity was certainly not a problem. The abbey at Pointe St-Mathieu is only a few short miles from the port of Brest. There seem to have been ships passing regularly from Brest to the British Isles, and especially directly to the northeastern English port of Newcastle-upon-Tyne, which is very close to the Scottish border. It would have been simplicity itself to load the St Matthew relic on such a ship and take it via Newcastle, or perhaps even more likely, bearing in mind security, directly to one of the ports on the Scottish east coast, of which there were, and are, many.

A more difficult issue is ownership. The monks of abbey St-Mathieu would have been extremely unlikely to simply hand over anything as precious as the very relic upon which their whole foundation was based. Simple theft seems highly unlikely, no matter how lax the monastic security might have been. We know that at the time Rosslyn Chapel was planned, Earl William Sinclair was not short of money, as mentioned in Chapter One, so it isn't entirely out of the question that he purchased the relic from the Duke of Brittany, in whose domains the monastery lay, but even this seems rather unlikely since monasteries usually fell beyond the control or influence of secular rulers.

Only someone with a great deal of influence – in fact, a person whose authority could not be questioned – could have persuaded the brothers of abbey St-Mathieu to part with something they had treasured for so long. Even a bishop or a cardinal of the Church might have been sidestepped or ignored, so in the end it came down to one individual. Only the Pope of the Roman Catholic Church or a highly placed and influential cardinal could, either openly or secretly, have ordered the relic of St Matthew to be placed into the hands of a person who would have been a stranger to both the abbey and to Brittany.

It was at this point that we thought back to our previous investigations, which at one stage had thrown up stories of a most remarkable individual by the name of Enea Silvio de' Piccolomini – better known to the world of the 15th century as Pope Pius II.

A Papal Connection

Judging by his early life, Enea Piccolomini must have been one of the least likely candidates to rise to the rank of ruler of the entire Catholic Church and a legatee of St Peter. Enea was born in October 1405 into a formerly rich, but at the time generally impoverished, family in Corsignano, Sienna, Italy. He showed early promise as a scholar and studied at the universities of

Sienna and Florence. The young Enea showed no inclination for the priesthood, and, from the very start of his manhood, he lived a life that was almost completely at odds with that expected of a parish priest, let alone a pope.

The fact was that Enea Piccolomini loved life, which he drank down like a heady wine. He soon became a writer and a noted poet and, in fact, has left behind a body of work unparalleled by anyone else who eventually rose to the Holy See. Working for various bishops and cardinals, Enea often became involved in papal intrigues, but he had a ready tongue, a sharp wit and boundless charm. This latter quality reflected itself in the fact that during his life he had at least two illegitimate children – which may not be surprising when one learns that much of his written fiction was of a deeply erotic, if also comic, nature. He was extremely well read, made it his business to meet many of the most famous scholars and political thinkers of his day, and he travelled extensively as an ambassador, a 'fixer' and almost certainly a spy.

In 1435, Enea Piccolomini found himself on yet another journey. At 30 years of age, he was sent by his then employer, Cardinal Albergati, to Scotland. He remained there for a number of months, during which time he was mixing freely with both royalty and aristocracy. It has to be admitted that nobody has any real clue as to why Piccolomini was visiting Scotland. In his own extensive memoirs he offers a number of possible reasons, none of which seem to hold much water, but whatever his mission might have been – open or clandestine – it did not prevent him from having a good time. He was personable, open, liberal and adaptable – all traits respected by modern-day Scots and so probably appreciated even back in the 15th century. Of the fact that he came into contact with Earl William Sinclair, we can have no doubt whatsoever because the two communicated years afterwards.

It was while Enea Piccolomini was in Scotland that he fathered one of his illegitimate children. He later told his own father in a letter that the child had died when a few months old, but he was almost certainly being sparing with the truth because local legend asserts that the child prospered and was adopted and brought up by none other than Earl William Sinclair.

Earl William should have been succeeded by what was supposed to be his eldest son, also called William, but for some odd reason this did not happen. Rather, his second son inherited and it has been suggested that this was because William Sinclair junior was not in fact a Sinclair at all but the result of Enea Piccolomini's over-amorous nature whilst he was resident in Scotland. There is absolutely no way of proving or disproving this assertion, but it cannot be denied that there seems to have been a bond of some sort between the two men that carried on after Piccolomini had returned to Italy. Perhaps Piccolomini's secret mission was to take the skull of St Matthew from Pointe St-Mathieu to the relative safety of Scotland. This is quite feasible considering that the man who charged him with this mission was the cardinal of the Basilica of the Holy Cross in Jerusalem in Rome, which famously held the Passion relics.

In a conversion to religion that makes St Paul's 'Road to Damascus' experience seem tame by comparison, Enea Piccolomini suddenly took holy orders around 1446 and began a meteoric rise that would see him elected as Pope in August 1458. It has to be said that in the six years he held the office, until his death in 1464, he made a real difference. He brought liberality and genuine humility to his years in the Vatican; increased the size of the Vatican library that had been started by his predecessor Pope Nicolas, fought against the slavery of children, sought to stop the progress of advancing Turkish forces in the East and achieved all of this with an originality that almost beggars belief. Catholic historians do not quite know what to make of Enea Piccolomini. The *Catholic Encyclopaedia* says of him:

> There have been widely divergent appreciations
> of the life of Pius II. While his varied talents and
> superior culture cannot be doubted, the motives
> of his frequent transfer of allegiance, the causes
> of the radical transformations which his opinions
> underwent, the influences exercised over him by
> the environment in which his lot was cast, are so
> many factors, the bearing of which can be justly and
> precisely estimated only with the greatest difficulty.

What cannot be denied is that at the time of his rise to the papacy, Enea Piccolomini was known to, and was almost undoubtedly a friend of, Earl William Sinclair of Rosslyn. The grant by the Scottish Royal Crown that gave William Sinclair the chance to build a new township – now known as Roslin – was signed in 1456. This was a necessary precursor to his intended building of Rosslyn Chapel, because he needed a trained workforce to undertake the task. Enea Piccolomini became Pope Pius II in 1458, but his influence in Rome had begun some time before. He had been a bishop since 1447, a favourite and confidant of two popes and became a cardinal in 1456.

Assuming the skull of St Matthew did eventually leave Brittany and arrive at Rosslyn, we have no way of knowing specifically when the event took place. Building Rosslyn Chapel was not a lightning process. Perhaps surprisingly for such a small structure it took 40 years to complete (though the richness of the stone carvings probably explains the protracted period). Is it possible that Rosslyn Chapel was indeed planned from the start to be a reliquary for the relics of St Matthew? Had Enea Piccolomini made some promise to Earl William Sinclair – perhaps in thanks for the Earl's assistance in sorting out his earlier parental problem? It is unlikely that we will ever know for certain. For reasons we will mention presently, the presence of the skull of St Matthew at Rosslyn Chapel, or indeed anywhere in Scotland, had to be kept a closely guarded secret, so if it came there at the hand or the instruction of Pope Pius II, it must have happened away from the glare of any public gaze.

One thing is certain: Rosslyn Chapel does not simply pay homage to its patron St Matthew, it is a veritable shrine to him and the stories of his life. It has never ceased to surprise us that at the time we began to dig deep into the history of this fascinating building, not a single local story or a half-remembered legend associated the mastery of the carvings with St Matthew's life. Yet there it is, for anyone to see. Every detail of the Christian tale of Myrna is present – even including the honey falling from above. The beehive was carefully and skilfully created and is unequivocal, yet until very recently it remained a total secret.

What is the use of an empty reliquary? The truth is that, like Sainte-Chapelle in Paris, it has no value, except as a glorious historical peculiarity. But whereas history positively shouts the presence in Sainte-Chapelle of some of the most stupendous relics of Christianity, there seems to be no proof at all that the skull of St Matthew was ever on display in Rosslyn Chapel. We are about to explain why its presence there could never be spoken about openly.

CHAPTER FOUR

In Dangerous Times

We had come to the conclusion that at least part of the reason for the creation of Rosslyn Chapel was to house the bones, and specifically the skull, of the Gospel writer and disciple St Matthew. Having come across the story about St Matthew's visit to, and martyrdom in, a city called Myrna, possibly Smyrna, now Izmir in Turkey, we were able to see how every detail of the story of the place and the miracle St Matthew performed there was played out amidst the stunning stone carving of the 15th-century Chapel. We thought it likely that the skull, kept for centuries near Brest in Brittany, had been obtained by Earl William Sinclair because of his friendship with Enea Silvio Piccolomini, who in 1458 became Pope Pius II.

Exactly *why* Earl William had wanted to create what amounted to a giant reliquary at his Midlothian home was undoubtedly a question we would have to address, but there was a more pressing issue to deal with if we were to convince ourselves that this remarkable story could be true. Generally speaking, any sort of reliquary, examples of which were made for many centuries, was fully intended to be seen and appreciated. But the same was also true of their contents. Saint's relics that still exist in various churches and cathedrals across the world are not always available to the faithful on a daily basis, but there are invariably times when any given relic is open to view. This is even true of the Shroud of Turin, which purports to be the cloth that covered the body of Jesus after his crucifixion. Genuine or not, as delicate as this ancient relic is, it is still taken out periodically for examination and adoration.

Such was not apparently the case at Rosslyn Chapel. There is no mention of the skull of St Matthew ever having been displayed there, except perhaps the reference to Earl William's 'secret', alluded to by Mary of Guise in the 16th century. This event may have inspired our curiosity and added to our incentive to do more research, but it could hardly be considered conclusive. So, if Earl William Sinclair had gone to so much obvious trouble to locate and obtain the revered skull, and then to create such an incredible home for it, why had he chosen to keep the fact a closely guarded secret? In fact the reason is not at all hard to discover and it lies at the heart of the country of Scotland and its difficult relationship with its southern neighbour, England.

The Origins of Great Britain

People looking at these islands from outside are used to referring to them as either Great Britain, or the United Kingdom. Because England, Scotland and Wales are glued together geologically, anyone might reasonably assume that they have always represented one indivisible unit, but nothing could be further from the truth. Going back all the way to Iron Age times, prior to the Roman invasion of Britain in AD 43, the British Isles were populated by a large number of disparate tribal groups. Most, if not all, of these could reasonably be contained within the general heading of Celtic people, but they were certainly not one cohesive nation. Even at the time the Romans crossed the English Channel and attempted to conquer the whole of the British Isles, many of the tribes living here maintained their own small kingdoms and regularly fought skirmishes or even long-term wars with their neighbours.

This state of affairs was initially useful to the Roman conquerors because they were able to use tribal differences as leverage, and the divide-and-conquer tactic in order to gain allies, but in the fullness of time it suited the Roman Empire to make the British Isles into one cohesive whole, all of which would rest under the Roman yoke.

Successive emperors succeeded in part at least. All of what is now England and Wales was eventually more or less subdued, but the same was never true in the case of the northernmost part of the British Isles, which is now Scotland. Meanwhile the whole of Ireland, both north and south, was left alone by the legions of Rome, who probably thought the effort necessary to placate them would not be sufficiently rewarded by the gains.

This was certainly the case with Scotland. The Romans did send punitive expeditions north, but they met with constant, stiff resistance in a mountainous and wild environment that the locals knew far better than the Romans did.

With little strategic or monetary value to gain from subduing Scotland, even if it had been possible to do so, the Romans were eventually content to build a long and impressive wall between the River Tyne and the Solway Firth and to consider this the most northerly extent of the Roman Empire. They had, in fact, tried to build a similar wall further north. The Antonine Wall was constructed in circa AD 140 on the orders of the Emperor Antoninus Pius; for a generation, it was the north-western frontier of the Roman Empire. It ran for 60km from modern Old Kilpatrick on the north side of the River Clyde to Bo'ness on the Firth of Forth. The experiment failed and the legions withdrew to what is now, more or less, the English and Scottish border. The new wall, known as Hadrian's Wall, was begun in AD 122 and remained in existence until the Roman legions withdrew from Britain in around AD 410.

The end of Roman Britain saw Scotland, and to a great extent Wales, in the hands of the original Celtic people who had inhabited the islands, whilst England was peopled by the Romano British, who were also Celts, but heavily influenced by several centuries of the Roman presence.

The lack of the legions for protection left England open to further invasions, this time by pagan tribes from the Continent. Initially, these invaders were Germanic in origin. One such group, the Angles, ultimately gave their name to the southern part of the British mainland in the name Angle Land, which eventually became England.

These Germanic people never managed to gain a foothold in Scotland, where the ferocious tribes had never lost the knack of fighting, as the English Celts had. The same was true in Wales, into which many of the remaining English Celts were pushed by the advancing Germanic tribes. As a result, both Scotland and Wales retained their Celtic identity, whereas England did not.

A new invasion, this time by the Norman French in 1066, saw England conquered more or less in its entirety. The Anglo Saxon kingdoms that had developed after the Roman retreat from Britain were subjugated by the Normans, and England gradually took on a new reality, far from its Celtic origins. The Norman kings were avaricious, greedy and suspicious, and soon set their sights on extending their influence out of England, into Wales, Ireland and Scotland. The Scots in particular had different ideas, and the seeds of a turbulent relationship between the two countries were sown, creating a perpetual series of skirmishes and battles that did not finally relent until the United Kingdom came into being in 1707 – and in some ways not even then.

Of course, England and Scotland were not at daggers drawn for the entire period. There were many years during which an uneasy truce existed and the Scots would probably have been happy for things to remain that way. Unfortunately, the Norman kings of England often saw things differently. The Normans were, by nature, a martial race and never seemed to be happy unless they were fighting a war against someone. This was particularly true of specific kings such as Edward I (1239–1307), who was King of the English between 1272 and 1307. Edward was a ferocious warlord who some might rightfully call a power-crazed control freak. He believed in a prophecy that said he would be king of many islands or lands. Edward simply could not leave either Wales or Scotland alone, and when he was not trying to interfere in the internal running of both kingdoms, he was at war with them.

Wales presented Edward with many problems, but by the end of his reign the English presence there was strong. Scotland was a different case altogether. A large proportion of the Scottish part of the British Isles is composed of mountainous country. Much of it was heavily wooded, and the Scots knew every twist and turn of their own domains. Even for Edward, who attracted the name 'Hammer of the Scots' (Malleus Scottorum), Scotland was no easy conquest. Nevertheless, he persevered, and when military might was not feasible or possible, he used political intrigue to gain his ends. He tried to emasculate the Scots as he had already achieved with the Welsh.

In 1296, Edward's insistence that *any* Scottish king should be subservient and owe fealty to himself, and further that Scotland should fight on behalf of England against France, led to open rebellion north of the border. As a result, Edward invaded Scotland. Whilst there, he stole what he *thought* was the Scottish coronation stone and also seized a number of important religious relics, including what was believed to be parts of the True Cross of Jesus (the Black Rood). It wasn't too long before the Scots had their revenge. In 1307, Edward I died and was succeeded by his far less successful son, Edward II. In the meantime, Scotland had a hero king in the form of Robert the Bruce. Under Robert's rule the Scots gradually won back all the land they had formerly lost to England, and in 1314 they inflicted a crushing blow on Edward II at the Battle of Bannockburn.

And so it went on, century after bloody century, with the more powerful England constantly making demands on Scotland, with which its citizens were unwilling to comply. On every occasion that English armies made forays into Scotland, more and more churches, castles and palaces were damaged or destroyed, more lives were lost and Scottish resistance to

England continued to harden. The tenacious Scots usually turned the tide in their favour eventually, but they could not get back all the religious items that Edward and other English kings had stolen. The areas of Scotland most prone to attack were on the borders and in the region around Scotland's capital, Edinburgh, including the area of Midlothian, where Rosslyn Chapel stands.

The Need for Secrecy

William Sinclair, Earl of Caithness and builder of Rosslyn Chapel, did not live in a particularly turbulent period as far as Scottish and English relations were concerned. There were battles at the beginning of the 1400s, and more would follow in 1513, especially at the Battle of Flodden, but generally speaking, during William's life, a sort of stalemate predominated. Not that this would have lulled anyone in Scotland into a false sense of security. If the English knew that a prize as valuable as the skull of St Matthew was to be found so far south in Scotland, they would have plundered the Chapel and stolen the relic at the next convenient opportunity.

If William Sinclair *did* manage to secure the priceless relic, it is easy to see why he would not have made the fact known to any but his most trusted intimates. Nor did the situation improve in successive generations. On the contrary – it got worse. By the time another William Sinclair was entertaining Mary of Guise in the 16th century, the relic was not only in danger from England but also from the fact that religion in Britain was changing dramatically. Calvinism had taken root in Scotland, and the whole Reformation movement was under way.

For many decades prior to the start of the 16th century, the Roman Catholic Church had been under attack – often from within its own ranks. It was accused of being lax, corrupt, greedy and completely out of touch with the very religion it was supposed to represent – namely Christianity. The situation had not been helped by a succession of popes and cardinals who were far more interested in their own wealth and status than they were in genuinely serving their flocks. The Christian populace was being fleeced wholesale by corrupt clergy, and whilst ordinary people starved for want of bread, churches, cathedrals and abbeys groaned under the weight of gold and silver.

Constant plagues and epidemics within communities across Europe and beyond led to a belief that humanity was clearly following the wrong religious path, and the Catholic Church was unable to counter such terrors, which protestors put down to the Church's own spiritual failings.

As printed books became available and the middle classes began to develop and become educated, more and more calls were made for the Church to reform itself. Unfortunately, this did not happen, and the inevitable result was open conflict between Rome and dissatisfied clergy who ultimately broke away from the Roman Catholic Church. Thus, the Reformation began, initially in Germany in 1517, but quite soon in many other places across Northern Europe. England broke with Rome as early as 1529, but this was not a truly Protestant revolt because the country retained a sort of English Catholicism for some time. Scotland was a different kettle of fish, and although it finally declared itself to Protestantism under law in 1560, efforts to overthrow Roman Catholicism had been underway for quite some time.

At the time Mary of Guise wrote her famous letter to Sir William Sinclair, in 1546, Protestant rumblings were already breaking out in Scotland. To those of intelligence it must have seemed as if the writing was on the wall. Mary of Guise herself was a staunch Roman Catholic, as was her daughter, Mary, Queen of Scots. As for Sir William and his Sinclair line, we will have more to say presently about what he and they most likely believed. All the same, at this time the relics of St Matthew were in danger on not one but two fronts. There was still always the possibility of an English invasion – and by this time the threat was as real as it had ever been. In addition, if Protestantism gained predominance in Scotland, which it did only a few years later, any saintly relic would be under threat – not of theft but of destruction this time.

Indeed, the relic could have been in great danger only a few years earlier. Henry VIII of England had decided that it would be useful if his young son, Edward, were to be betrothed to Mary of Guise's infant daughter, Mary, Queen of Scots. Mary of Guise would have none of the suggestion: she hated Henry. Years earlier, whilst between wives, he had mooted that Mary of Guise would make a good match for him. She had quipped that she had only a slender neck and therefore could not marry Henry. This related to the fact that Henry had beheaded his second wife, Anne Boleyn.

Instead of choosing young Edward, Mary of Guise betrothed her daughter to the son of the King of France. Henry was furious and decided to invade Scotland, in order to force the betrothal to take place. This episode was known as the Rough Wooing, and in 1544 Rosslyn Castle was badly damaged by the forces of the English Earl of Hereford, who tried to burn it to the ground. History is silent as to their treatment of the nearby Chapel, but it seems to have survived intact on that occasion. It may not have fared so well if it was generally known that such a precious relic was housed there.

In truth, there had been no period between the founding of Rosslyn Chapel and Mary of Guise's correspondence with Sir William Sinclair when it would have been safe to admit to the world at large that the skull of the blessed St Matthew was housed in its own fabulous reliquary at Rosslyn. What is more, there never would be such a time until the relatively modern era. By the late 19th century, the situation had changed for other reasons, and it is possible that all knowledge of the existence of the skull had been forgotten – or else, at some time during the intervening period, it had been moved elsewhere.

Not only would the relic have had to be kept secret, it would also have needed to be kept safe and secure. The skull itself would have been housed in a reliquary of some sort, and we have no idea how large this was or even what it might have looked like. We could certainly expect that it would have been made of gold and was most likely of exquisite workmanship. Under normal circumstances during this period, treasures of great worth, together with gold and silver coinage, tended to be kept in castles. This was one of the major functions of medieval castles, at the heart of which would have been a strongroom, heavily fortified and perpetually guarded, in which secure chests would have held the money. The Sinclairs had their own castle, just a few hundred metres from Rosslyn Chapel, but as we have just seen, Rosslyn Castle was often the focus of attack and possible destruction. In any case, logically, the relic of St Matthew would be kept somewhere in the reliquary that had been created for it.

The Secret Vault

This brings us to a discussion of the supposed 'vault' that exists somewhere within or under Rosslyn Chapel or possibly even the Castle. Strong and enduring legends in the area speak of a tradition in which sons of the Sinclair family of Rosslyn would be buried in a vault within the Chapel – in full battle armour. There seems to be little doubt that this story is true, but it also appears that the location of this vault was eventually forgotten, or perhaps not passed on to the survivors of the family. Such a state of affairs might seem unlikely were it not for the fact that in 1780 the Sinclair line died out and was replaced by the nearest living relatives who took on the name Erskine-Sinclair. In 1837, the second Earl of Rosslyn, premier member of the Erskine-Sinclair family, died, having left a request to be buried in the vault, alongside his predecessors, the mediaeval Sinclair earls. The problem was that, search as they might, nobody could locate the vault. They investigated the Chapel thoroughly for a week, but no entrance was found to the burial vault.

Floor slabs were lifted and holes were made in masonry, and although signs of non-aristocratic burials did exist under the Chapel's floor, not a trace of any earl, reposed in his armour, was to be found anywhere, and neither was the entrance to the reported crypt. In the end, the Erskine-Sinclair Earl in question was buried alongside his wife, in the main altar in the Lady Chapel. Does this mean that no such vault ever existed and that the whole thing was nothing but a myth? This seems improbable for two reasons.

Firstly, we have no idea where the earls of old were buried – and they must have been laid to rest somewhere. Secondly, we have an incident that took place in the 17th century, during the bloody period known as the English Civil War, but which also heavily affected Scotland.

The English Civil War was fought between the forces of King Charles I and those of England's Parliament. It began in 1642 and was waged, on and off, until 1651. After the execution of King Charles I in 1649, hostilities did not cease, and in 1650 English forces under General Monk entered Scotland. There they fought a battle against the Scots at Dunbar, not far from Rosslyn Chapel. During the Battle of Dunbar, John Sinclair of Rosslyn was killed. He had previously requested burial in his full armour with the Sinclair earls at the Chapel; his wish was granted and he was buried within the vault, after which the vault entrance was sealed and concealed.

Only a week after the Battle of Dunbar, the English forces approached Rosslyn and took possession of the Chapel. By this time, John Sinclair had been buried with his ancestors, in full battle armour, apparently without any difficulty. He had certainly not been laid to rest in the land outside the Chapel and there was no trace of a grave within. John Sinclair was said to be the last Sinclair to be buried in this fashion, but it is clear that, in the 17th century, knowledge of the vault and how to access it still existed. Considering the short space of time between his death and the Chapel being captured by the English, access to the family vault must have been fairly straightforward.

We know that during the Victorian renovations of the Chapel in the 19th century, the Chapel floor was lifted, but no trace of the missing vault was found at this time. Our knowledge of the existence of the vault dates back to the work of Father Richard Augustine Hay, who researched Rosslyn Chapel and the Sinclair genealogies and wrote extensively about it at the start of the 18th century. His work was somewhat fanciful, and he stated that there were extensive tunnels under the Chapel, also making the suggestion that within these chambers 12 Sinclair knights, in their armour, have been sleeping, ready to come to Scotland's aid should they be needed in the future. On the other hand, are they protecting something for posterity? In reality, the 12 Templar knights almost certainly owe more to a fanciful writer than to historical fact.

✠ · ✠ · ✠

John Ritchie knew of a group of American naval personnel who, in the 1970s, brought ground detection equipment from Holy Loch in Scotland to the Rosslyn Chapel site. John saw the results of this survey, which definitely indicated that there were tunnels in the area, running away from Rosslyn Chapel. Perhaps one or more of these tunnels once led from the Chapel to Rosslyn Castle, and it is quite likely that one of these carries the Sinclair earls' vault. Within this labyrinth, Earl William Sinclair and the other stewards of Rosslyn Chapel would no doubt have kept the relic of St Matthew.

The only puzzle that remains is how access was gained from the Chapel to the tunnels and vault. We know this cannot be via the floor of the Chapel itself because that has been lifted on more than one occasion and no entrance was found. The crypt is a more likely candidate. It is at the east end of the Chapel and is approached by a flight of steep stairs from a position to the south of the altar. The crypt (or more properly the sacristy) may represent part of an earlier structure than the Chapel, as some historians claim. This earlier structure could have been deliberately incorporated into the Chapel we see today; or indeed, the chamber could also be in the Castle rather than the Chapel.

Although intriguing in its own right, there is no indication of an obvious entrance from the sacristy to any subterranean chamber. Three-dimensional scans of the Chapel, taken by representatives of Historic Scotland in 2010, also failed to locate the tunnels or a vault, but that is not particularly surprising because this survey did not go below ground level.

The evidence we have, particularly that relating to the aftermath of the Battle of Dunbar in 1650, indicates that to those who knew how to access the vault, the procedure cannot have been particularly arduous and certainly did not involve any major demolition and rebuilding. The fact that Sir William Sinclair could show the relic to Mary of Guise in the 16th century also seems to indicate that if the relic was kept in or adjacent to the Sinclair earls' vault, it was not impossible to access.

Not only do we remain absolutely confident that the vault and accompanying tunnels *do* exist, we are also sure that we know how and where they were entered. It was never too difficult for those in the know to access the vault and, like so much else associated with Rosslyn Chapel, the entrance is hidden in plain sight. Accessing it did not involve knocking through any walls, but it was probably only ever known to the earls and their most intimate servants.

We can thank John for realizing where the vault and the entrance of the tunnels beneath the Chapel must be. He has probably spent as many hours within Rosslyn Chapel as any living individual. His knowledge of the structure is unparalleled, and he has taken literally thousands of photographs of every possible niche and corner of the building. John shared his reasoning with me, and together we weighed up the evidence carefully. In the end, there can be no other explanation, but just as all knowledge of the St Matthew–Myrna connection has remained a completely open mystery throughout so many centuries, so has all the necessary information regarding the entrance to the vault and tunnels.

During the research and planning of this, our second book, we have talked long and hard about the situation, wondering whether it would be right or fair to divulge this particular secret of Rosslyn Chapel. In the end, we decided that, for now at least, the secret should remain. In any case, it would ultimately be the responsibility of the custodians of Rosslyn Chapel to locate and open the vault, and of course it has to be remembered that the vault contains Christian burials in sanctified ground. In any case, we are of the opinion that if all the treasures *were* uncovered, much of the intriguing mystery of Rosslyn Chapel would be gone – and what would our world be without mysteries?

Was the earls' vault the place where the skull of St Matthew was kept safe, initially from the marauding English and later from the forces of the Reformation? It seems possible, though bearing in mind the likelihood that the Chapel was primarily built for the relic, it is also likely that the skull of Matthew always had a chamber of its own, perhaps accessed from the same entrance. Is the supposed skull of one of Christianity's most famous and yet hardly known characters still sleeping away the centuries where it was left by the last Sinclair earl who gazed upon it? Most probably it is, but there is another, even more tantalizing possibility that we will deal with later in the book.

CHAPTER FIVE

Renaissance Men

Rosslyn Chapel was built at the start of a period of European history that is generally referred to as the Renaissance. The word is often bandied around, but what exactly was the Renaissance and how could it have had a bearing on Scotland or an aristocratic family such as that of the Sinclairs?

In its most tangible form the Renaissance, which began roughly in the 14th century, is recognized by the wonderful flowering of art that emerged, and for this reason it is towards the arts that most people look when discussing the Renaissance – in other words, it is often taken to have been a wholly artistic phenomenon. Nothing could be further from the truth. Ultimately, artistic advancement depended on a number of other factors, not least of which were rich patrons who could supply the money necessary for artists to spend weeks, months or years on particular projects. The fact that patrons wished to support artists so liberally tells its own story about what the Renaissance really was – a search for knowledge, made possible because of changing religious ideals as well as altering social and economic circumstances. In its totality the Renaissance ultimately changed the world significantly, setting humanity on a course that would eventually lead to the world we know today.

Few historians would dispute that the Renaissance began in Italy, for a series of very specific reasons. After the fall of the classical Roman Empire, Italy was broken into a number of different regions and, in fact, never achieved the status of a united nation until comparatively recent times. These regions, or states, were still heavily affected by the Roman Empire, and some of them responded to a way of thinking that had predominated throughout the days of the Empire – namely a profound distrust of kings. It might seem strange when one considers the series of all-powerful emperors that Roman citizens generally had a fear and even a loathing of monarchy, but this had been evident right back to the days of Julius Caesar and is one explanation why so many emperors met a grizzly fate. Dynastic kingship was anathema to Rome and created a mindset that continued long after the Roman Empire had crumbled to dust.

It might not be too surprising then to learn that some of the powerful city-states that gradually emerged in Italy, from the 12th century on, represented examples of the modern world's earliest republics. Two of the most influential and powerful were Florence and Venice.

Italians had always been great traders. Even when the Empire had disintegrated, Italy stood in a very good position regarding trade routes across Western Europe and well beyond. It projected into the Mediterranean, giving it access to Eastern markets, but was also connected via seaways and road links through the Alps to northwestern Europe – in particular the lucrative wool trade that flourished in Flanders, which in turn relied on British wool.

Freed from the constraining hand of feudalism that still predominated across most of Europe, the city-states of Italy paved the way for a rising middle class to develop – something that did not take place further north until much later. Powerful families began to emerge, especially in Florence and Venice. They grew wealthy on trade and had an unsurprisingly cosmopolitan attitude to life. With both time and money to spare, it was probably quite natural that these families would choose to surround themselves with luxury, which was one of the reasons why artists found generous patrons in the city-states of Italy. However, the climate was right for something else to take place, and this also sprang out of the same influential families in the Italian republics. It was a desire for knowledge and education.

No family can lay greater claim to the Renaissance than that of the Medici, which represented an extremely wealthy and influential Florentine dynasty. It might be suggested that the founder of the Renaissance was Cosimo de Medici (1389–1464). So powerful was this man it is suggested that during his life Cosimo de Medici was King of Florence in everything but name. The family fortunes had come from wool, and by the time Cosimo was born, the Medici were already the most powerful family in Florence. If Cosimo were, in reality, either a king or a dictator, he was certainly a benign one. He once said: 'In my life I have spent my time earning and spending money – but spending money has always brought me the greatest satisfaction.' Cosimo instigated a college for the study of the Classics, as well as laying the foundations for the greatest library that had ever belonged to an individual, though this library was not exclusive and was available to any interested student. He was a great patron of the arts, but in most cases commissioned structures, sculptures and paintings that would be seen by most, if not all, Florentines, and he strove hard to reconcile the differences between the Italian states – and by so doing also sought to limit the influence other nations would have on the Italian peninsula.

In short, the presence of families like that of Cosimo de Medici consolidated the Italian republics. They were fiercely independent and sometimes warlike, but they revered knowledge for its own sake; and though they paid lip service to the Catholic Church, they were not restricted in the subjects they chose to study. Most significantly of all, they collected books, which they rightfully saw as being the repositories of knowledge.

Books and Libraries

It cannot be overstressed just how expensive books were in the pre-printing era. Every book had to be meticulously copied by hand. Not only was the copying of books extremely time-consuming, it also relied on expensive materials such as vellum and leather. Most were not simply pages of text, but were, in themselves, great works of art. Books were highly decorated (illuminated) and had been more or less the sole prerogative of the Church. Religious books, plus a few secular ones, had usually been produced in the scriptoriums of monasteries, where individual monks could spend years working on a single volume. The Church was quite jealous of its virtual monopoly in book making, and it isn't surprising because the Roman Catholic Church had a vested interest in making sure that the information available in books was only utilized by the Church itself – or by extremely wealthy patrons who kept religious works for their own use.

Throughout the Middle Ages, across all of Europe, ordinary people were definitely not encouraged to read; not just the Church but also secular rulers understood very well that with education could come dissatisfaction – and eventually revolution. Feudalism depended on everything staying more or less the way it had always been. Everyone knew their place within society and did not expect to rise beyond a certain level that had been prescribed by the circumstances of their birth.

In the counting houses and mercantile halls of 14th-century Italy, things were rather different. If merchants were to prosper and flourish, they needed to be both numerate and literate. All manner of documents had to be produced and understood – even by comparatively lowly individuals. But most important of all, they were not subject to the regulations of the Church regarding what could or could not be read.

A factor that definitely helped Cosimo de Medici, and his successor Lorenzo (known as 'the Magnificent'), to gather together what eventually became the most famed library of its day, was the fall of Constantinople (modern Istanbul in Turkey) which was the centre of Eastern Christianity. For some time prior to the 15th century, it had been under threat from Islamic forces pushing ever closer. Although Constantinople itself did not fall to Islam until 1453, the writing had been on the wall for some time. Many of the Eastern Christians moved west, especially to Italy, and all manner of priceless manuscripts, especially those relating to the Classical philosophers, found their way into the hands of private collectors such as the Medici. Books also found their way to Italy from North

Africa, affected not only by the study of the Classics but also by learned Arab scholars.

Another factor that helped to spur on the Renaissance was a short but very important excursion on the part of the Vatican into a form of liberalism that had never been seen before. In 1447, a man by the name of Tommaso Parentucelli was elected Pope. He took the name Nicholas V, and although he only occupied the Holy See for eight years, he demonstrated his humanist leanings and his liberal attitude time and again. Most importantly, he was a book collector in his own right and began what was eventually to be one of the most famous libraries in the world, at the Vatican itself. He amassed over 1,600 books, which was a colossal amount at the time, and he also mixed with other book collectors and encouraged their efforts, too.

A few years later, in 1458, the Pope elected to fill the vacant throne of Peter was Pius II, none other than the same Enea Piccolomini, who had visited Scotland earlier in his life and who was a friend of Sir William Sinclair, builder of Rosslyn Chapel. Pius II was a great supporter and patron of the arts, and being a poet and writer himself, was a true intellectual. He greatly expanded the Vatican library and also corresponded with other bibliophiles. Throughout his time in the Vatican, like Nicholas V, he held back the cruel hand of the Inquisition and sought to portray Christianity in the light of his own humanist leanings. Perhaps inevitably, the actions of Nicholas V and Pius II led to a backlash, which saw a much more conservative group of pontiffs taking command thereafter. Had this not been the case, perhaps the forces of Protestantism that effectively destroyed the Roman Catholic Church in northwestern Europe may never have gained the upper hand.

Good King René

Yet another boost to the Renaissance came during the 15th century from René of Anjou, King of Naples, Duke of Anjou and Count of Provence. Despite his list of multinational titles, René was brought up in Lorraine, France. He underwent many trials and tribulations during his life, was frequently imprisoned and eventually lost his holdings in Italy, but through all of this René remained one of the most cultured rulers of the entire period. Being both a poet and writer of books himself, René was also a talented painter, a patron of artists and a prolific bibliophile. His Italian contacts made it possible for him to solicit manuscripts from within Italy itself and also from further east, and throughout most of his life René was also on very good terms with the French Crown, which, thanks to Charles VII's own love of books, meant a mutual expanding of libraries in the West.

It is surely certain that René d'Anjou regularly met Sir Gilbert Haye, the Scot who would go on to become Earl William Sinclair's librarian, but who had been a Chamberlain and librarian to King Charles VII of France for many years. René knew the Medici and also had dealings with popes regarding volumes in the Vatican library, and it was in these illustrious circles that Sir Gilbert Haye moved for a couple of decades or more.

We know from his own writings that Sir Gilbert Haye was well travelled, and we can take it as a fact that he had undertaken journeys to secure ever more volumes for the library of King Charles VII. There is no definitive proof that Gilbert ever visited Florence or Venice, but it is extremely likely that he did. What all of this means is that by the time Gilbert Haye returned to Scotland to work for Earl William Sinclair, he had important contacts all over Europe and beyond, as well as writing a number of books of his own and translating many others.

There are a number of reasons why we know that the Sinclair earls definitely *were* avid collectors of books. In 1452, a domestic fire broke out in Rosslyn Castle, and there is a long and quite amusing story of how the Earl and his staff managed to save his books by throwing them from an upstairs window to waiting hands below. In addition, many of the works from the Sinclair library found their way into private collections, whilst five of them, in this case dating back to 1488, are to be found in the National Library of Scotland. Another sizeable collection is presently in the Bodleian Library in Oxford, England, having been seized during the English Civil War by Lord Thomas Fairfax and later donated to Oxford University. The fact that some of these books, plus examples of the ones still in Scotland, are from a date later than the life of Earl William Sinclair demonstrates that the habit of collecting books and building up the Sinclair library was passed on by William to his own children.

The founding of this library is undoubtedly thanks to the presence and knowledge of Sir Gilbert Haye – a Renaissance man if ever there was one, but it is not the only reason why the age of liberality and learning came so early to Scotland. Another part of the story relates to Scotland's physical position and its troubled relations with its more powerful southern neighbour, England.

The Auld Alliance

As we have observed, Scotland was often seen as a winnable prize by kings of England, especially the early Norman kings. Under such circumstances, and fiercely opposed to English domination in their own lands, it is not surprising that the Scots turned their gaze in other directions for powerful allies that might assist them in fending off the English threat. In particular, Scotland formed a close and lasting tie with France.

As early as 1295, a treaty was signed between John Balliol of Scotland and Philip IV of France, during the time when Scotland was being perpetually threatened and harassed by Edward I of England. Under this treaty, both countries agreed that should either be attacked by England, the other would immediately come to its defence by invading England. France, a country that was infinitely larger and more powerful than Scotland, had its own reasons for being interested in such an alliance. From the very start of Norman dominance in England, right back to 1066, kings of England had also considered themselves to be kings of large areas of what is now France, together with the French territories proper, around Paris. A number of wars were fought in which the English invaded France, and it would have suited French monarchs to know that any such invasion would lead to a Scottish invasion of England, leaving the Norman kings fighting a war on two entirely different fronts.

By 1326, the original treaty was renewed by King Robert the Bruce, and it was invoked again on no less than six occasions up until the 15th century. So close did the political and economic ties between Scotland and France become, and so long-lasting, that in Scottish parlance they became known as the 'Auld Alliance'. This 'special bond' was in operation fully at the time of the life of Earl William Sinclair, and indeed the time spent in France, working specifically for its king, Charles VII, shows that the career of Sir Gilbert Haye flourished *because of* the Auld Alliance.

Nor was the special relationship between Scotland and France restricted to a military alliance. For many centuries Scotland traded directly with France, and also many other states on the Continent of Europe. The Scots, like the rest of the British, are a maritime nation and have always relied on trade, in order to sell the surplus of what they could make and grow for what they could not. The Scots were active in the wine trade, which extended to Portugal and Spain. Scottish wool, like that in England, was shipped to Flanders and France and then onward to Italy. Dried and salted fish caught off the coast of Scotland and prepared on the east coast, eventually formed a staple for Friday-conscious Christians in France and down into the Mediterranean.

Aside from trade there were cultural ties. It is said that as recently as the 17th century one could readily hear French being spoken on the streets of Edinburgh and other Scottish towns and cities. Educated Scots often went to French universities or, like Sir Gilbert Haye, found employment with the rich and powerful in France. Meanwhile a number of structures in Scotland, including some of its most enduring castles, were heavily influenced by the French taste in architecture – likewise some of Scotland's churches.

So trusted were the Scots in France that, for centuries, the King of France's personal bodyguards were made up of Scots soldiers, the 'Garde Ecosse', formed from the sons of Scotland's premier families. To a great extent, this special relationship was one of convenience as far as Scotland was concerned, but it existed and was sincerely felt by both parties.

Given this constant traffic between Scotland and France, not to mention other countries in Europe, it is not surprising that the effects of the gradually developing Renaissance were felt keenly north of the border. The Renaissance, and all it offered, suited the Scottish mentality. Scots were far from being the downtrodden Anglo Saxons further south, who were subjugated and beaten into feudal servitude by the ferocious Norman kings. They had, since time out of mind, developed the attitude for which other nations, especially the Cretans, also became famous. Their motto was 'better dead than a slave', and in their present fight for independence from the United Kingdom the Scots show amply that their desire for self-determination remains as solid as ever.

This attitude was expressed as early as 1320 in a very famous document sent to the Pope by the people of Scotland. It is known as the Declaration of Arbroath. At the time, the Scots were being constantly attacked and interfered with by the English, partially due to the excommunication of King Robert the Bruce and Scotland itself. It was felt in Scotland that Rome had shown a disproportionate regard for the feelings of the English and had not fully taken into account either the wishes or the needs of the Scots, who considered themselves to be just as deserving of the Pope's attention and sympathy.

Scotland's Most Important Declaration

The Declaration of Arbroath, which actually represents a letter to the Pope, was most probably written by Bernard of Kilwinning, the former abbot of Kilwinning and a Tironensian (a monastic order which we will have more to say about later). It was signed by a long list of the great and good of Scotland's aristocracy, including the Sinclair Lord of the time and also the grandfather of Sir Gilbert Haye (who had the same name and was Constable of Scotland).

The fact that the Scots were pleading to the Pope for better treatment and a greater consideration is not what makes the document so interesting, but the *wording*, which says so much about what the Scots believed regarding kingship and the freedom of the individual. We reproduce it below so that readers can judge for themselves the sort of people the Scots were, back in the 14th century. At the same period, most of those living south of the border were locked into feudal serfdom, with never a thought that they may in any way be able to *choose* who ruled them or what their king's political strategy might be.

> To the most Holy Father and Lord in Christ,
> the Lord John, by divine providence Supreme
> Pontiff of the Holy Roman and Universal Church,
> his humble and devout sons Duncan, Earl of
> Fife, Thomas Randolph, Earl of Moray, Lord of
> Man and of Annandale, Patrick Dunbar, Earl of
> March, Malise, Earl of Strathearn, Malcolm, Earl
> of Lennox, William, Earl of Ross, Magnus, Earl
> of Caithness and Orkney, and William, Earl of

Sutherland; Walter, Steward of Scotland, William Soules, Butler of Scotland, James, Lord of Douglas, Roger Mowbray, David, Lord of Brechin, David Graham, Ingram Umfraville, John Menteith, guardian of the earldom of Menteith, Alexander Fraser, Gilbert Haye, Constable of Scotland, Robert Keith, Marischal of Scotland, Henry St Clair, John Graham, David Lindsay, William Oliphant, Patrick Graham, John Fenton, William Abernethy, David Wemyss, William Mushet, Fergus of Ardrossan, Eustace Maxwell, William Ramsay, William Mowat, Alan Murray, Donald Campbell, John Cameron, Reginald Cheyne, Alexander Seton, Andrew Leslie, and Alexander Straiton, and the other barons and freeholders and the whole community of the realm of Scotland send all manner of filial reverence, with devout kisses of his blessed feet.

Most Holy Father and Lord, we know and from the chronicles and books of the ancients we find that among other famous nations our own, the Scots, has been graced with widespread renown. They journeyed from Greater Scythia by way of the Tyrrhenian Sea and the Pillars of Hercules, and dwelt for a long course of time in Spain among the most savage tribes, but nowhere could they be subdued by any race, however barbarous. Thence they came, twelve hundred years after the people of Israel crossed the Red Sea, to their home in the west where they still live today. The Britons they first drove out, the Picts they utterly destroyed, and, even though very often assailed by the Norwegians, the Danes and the English, they took possession of that home with many victories and untold efforts; and, as the historians of old time bear witness, they have held it free of all bondage ever since. In their kingdom there have reigned one hundred and thirteen kings of their own royal stock, the line unbroken by a single foreigner.

The high qualities and deserts of these people, were they not otherwise manifest, gain glory enough from this: that the King of kings and Lord of lords, our Lord Jesus Christ, after His Passion and Resurrection, called them, even though settled in the uttermost parts of the earth, almost the first to His most holy faith. Nor would He have them confirmed in that faith by merely anyone but by the first of His Apostles – by calling, though second or third in rank – the most gentle Saint Andrew, the Blessed Peter's brother, and desired him to keep them under his protection as their patron forever.

The Most Holy Fathers your predecessors gave careful heed to these things and bestowed many favours and numerous privileges on this same kingdom and people, as being the special charge of the Blessed Peter's brother. Thus our nation under their protection did indeed live in freedom and peace up to the time when that mighty prince the King of the English, Edward, the father of the one who reigns today, when our kingdom had no head and our people harboured no malice or treachery and were then unused to wars or invasions, came in the guise of a friend and ally to harass them as an enemy. The deeds of cruelty, massacre, violence, pillage, arson, imprisoning prelates, burning down monasteries, robbing and killing monks and nuns, and yet other outrages without number which he committed against our people, sparing neither age nor sex, religion nor rank, no one could describe nor fully imagine unless he had seen them with his own eyes.

But from these countless evils we have been set free, by the help of Him Who though He afflicts yet heals and restores, by our most tireless Prince, King and Lord, the Lord Robert. He, that his people and his heritage might be delivered out of the hands of our enemies, met toil and fatigue, hunger and peril, like another Macabaeus or Joshua and bore them cheerfully. Him, too, divine providence, his right of succession according to or laws and customs which we shall maintain to the death, and the due consent and assent of us all have made our Prince and King. To him, as to the man by whom salvation has been wrought unto our people, we are bound both by law and by his merits that our freedom may be still maintained, and by him, come what may, we mean to stand.

Yet if he should give up what he has begun, and agree to make us or our kingdom subject to the King of England or the English, we should exert ourselves at once to drive him out as our enemy and a subverter of his own rights and ours, and make some other man who was well able to defend us our King; for, as long as but a hundred of us remain alive, never will we on any conditions be brought under English rule. It is in truth not for glory, nor riches, nor honours that we are fighting, but for freedom – for that alone, which no honest man gives up but with life itself.

Therefore it is, Reverend Father and Lord, that we beseech your Holiness with our most earnest prayers and suppliant hearts, inasmuch as you will in your sincerity and goodness consider all this, that, since with Him Whose Vice-Regent on earth you are there is neither weighing nor distinction of Jew and Greek, Scotsman or Englishman, you will look with the eyes of a father on the troubles and privation brought by the English upon us and upon the Church of God. May it please you to admonish and exhort the King of the English, who ought to be satisfied with what belongs to him since England used once to be enough for seven kings or more, to leave us Scots in peace, who live in this poor little Scotland, beyond which there is no dwelling-place at all, and covet nothing but our own. We are sincerely willing to do anything for him, having regard to our condition, that we can, to win peace for ourselves.

This truly concerns you, Holy Father, since you see the savagery of the heathen raging against the Christians, as the sins of Christians have indeed deserved, and the frontiers of Christendom being

pressed inward every day; and how much it will
tarnish your Holiness's memory if (which God
forbid) the Church suffers eclipse or scandal in any
branch of it during your time, you must perceive.
Then rouse the Christian princes who for false
reasons pretend that they cannot go to help of the
Holy Land because of wars they have on hand with
their neighbours. The real reason that prevents them
is that in making war on their smaller neighbours
they find quicker profit and weaker resistance. But
how cheerfully our Lord the King and we too would
go there if the King of the English would leave us
in peace, He from Whom nothing is hidden well
knows; and we profess and declare it to you as the
Vicar of Christ and to all Christendom.

But if your Holiness puts too much faith in the
tales the English tell and will not give sincere belief
to all this, nor refrain from favouring them to our
prejudice, then the slaughter of bodies, the perdition
of souls, and all the other misfortunes that will
follow, inflicted by them on us and by us on them,
will, we believe, be surely laid by the Most High to
your charge.

To conclude, we are and shall ever be, as far as
duty calls us, ready to do your will in all things,
as obedient sons to you as His Vicar; and to Him
as the Supreme King and Judge we commit the
maintenance of our cause, casting our cares upon
Him and firmly trusting that He will inspire us with
courage and bring our enemies to nought.

May the Most High preserve you to his Holy
Church in holiness and health and grant you length
of days.

Given at the monastery of Arbroath in Scotland
on the sixth day of the month of April in the year of
grace thirteen hundred and twenty and the fifteenth
year of the reign of our King aforesaid.

Surviving as it has on the northern frontiers of Europe,
Scotland was never a rich nation. Most of its inhabitants lived
a life based on subsistence farming, yet in its cities it cultivated
an appreciation of art and a fondness for learning that could
equal that of any other nation in Europe. Its political ideals, its
insistence on freedom – in every sense of the word – and the
raw truthfulness of its people meant that it responded quickly
and positively to the humanism and liberalism that character-
ized the arrival of the Renaissance. Scotland became a centre of
learning very early. The University of St Andrews is one of the
oldest universities in Europe, having been first established in
1410, and this was far from being the only centre of education.

We know little about the educational background of Earl
William Sinclair, the builder of Rosslyn Chapel, but we can
take it as certain that he was a cultured, well-versed individual,
who was not only fully literate, but who revelled in French and
Latin books – which were so important to him that when a
fire broke out in his castle, he was willing to risk his very life
to rescue them. Sir William moved in the court of the Scottish
King, where he held a hereditary title, earned by his family
from so many generations of loyalty. He would have met all
of the famous people of his day who visited Scotland and he

may well have travelled to the continent himself. And as if to prove just how important education and learning was to him, he employed one of the brightest and most intellectual individuals available to educate his own children and to assist him in his own burst of creativity.

It was out of the beliefs and aspirations of Earl William Sinclair and Sir Gilbert Haye combined that Rosslyn Chapel sprang, and whereas many baronial families of the period sought to gain favour with the Almighty by dedicating churches, it is clear that Rosslyn Chapel was something very different. It was not simply born out of religious zeal, but it was also an experiment in changing values and a representation in stone of the fountain of knowledge that was pouring into Scotland at the time. It was, effectively, a scriptorium in stone, designed to educate and to preserve arcane knowledge.

Rosslyn Chapel stands at an important crossroads. In many respects, as a sacred reliquary and a portrayal in stone of the life of a semi-mythical saint, the building seems old-fashioned, appearing as it did at the threshold of a completely new era. But this squat little structure is truly an enigma in stone, and we have learned that nothing about it can be taken at face value. Its components have to be meticulously teased apart if we are ever going to be able to put ourselves into the mindset of its creators. When this exercise is undertaken, and even when all the fanciful 19th-century legends and 21st-century speculations are dismissed, what remains has the power to shock and surprise us on an almost daily basis.

CHAPTER SIX

A View to the East

W hen we first began researching and then writing about Rosslyn Chapel, we each brought our own particular experience to bear on the building and those who had created it. Part of Alan's knowledge came from years of studying ancient cultures and their understanding of astronomy, especially in the British Isles. We were aware that there were many occasions on which the first Christians in the British Isles had deliberately placed their churches on sites that had already been revered for countless centuries. Persistent rumours suggested that this was the case with Rosslyn, and that the site of the Chapel was once that of a Megalithic structure such as a standing stone or perhaps a stone circle. Bearing in mind the physical placement of Rosslyn Chapel on the landscape, this seemed extremely likely.

Alan had written extensively, both in partnership with others and alone, about the feats and knowledge of the late Stone Age and Bronze Age people from the far west of Europe. In particular, Alan was always fascinated by many of the structures from the period that are still to be found all over these islands. Most are made of mammoth pieces of stone, found on the landscape or quarried for the purpose. These were carefully sourced, pounded into shape and dragged, sometimes great distances across the landscape, to be erected into circles, avenues, alignments or as single, standing stones.

With no written evidence from such a remote period, it is left to us to try and understand why our long-dead ancestors went to such trouble to make certain that these often massive stones were placed with such care and precision. Sad to say, because of religious prejudice, many of the great stone monuments that once existed in the southern British Isles were destroyed over the centuries, or else plundered for building stone. This had not happened to the same extent in the Celtic homelands of Wales, Ireland and especially Scotland. It is possible that successive generations in these places felt a kindred spirit with those who had laboured so long and with such obvious fervour to leave these impressive legacies on the landscape, or it could simply be that the Celts, being a naturally superstitious people, thought it best to leave the leviathans in stone where they were.

Although antiquarians of the modern period, especially from the 18th century, showed a great interest in the standing stones and stone circles, they had little idea *who* had created them and even less regarding *why* they should have been made in the first place. Great structures such as Stonehenge in southern England were generally considered to have been the work of the Romans, and though successive generations of investigators soon came to realize that this cannot have been the case and that such feats of engineering were much older than the Roman period, their true purpose remained a mystery until comparatively recently.

The Research of Alexander Thom

One man who was determined to discover exactly what was going through the minds of the Neolithic farmers when they planned and built so many circles and avenues across the British Isles was a Scot. His name was Alexander Thom, and he was born in March 1894 on the west coast of Scotland at Carradale in Argyll. Thom's father was an intelligent and hard-working farmer, and he instilled a strong work ethic into his son Alexander, who, possessing a naturally practical streak, took up engineering, rising eventually to be Professor of Engineering at Oxford University in England.

Thom had two abiding interests outside of his professional career. He was a keen sailor and, perhaps in part because of this, also an avid and knowledgeable amateur astronomer. As a young man, whilst sailing around the coast of Scotland, he had often seen standing stones and stone circles – particularly those on the island of Orkney – and he began to wonder if part of the reason why they had been so laboriously created had been astronomical. In particular, he formulated the theory that many of the Scottish stone circles, most of which are within view of the sea, had been built in order to gain a better understanding of the complex behaviour of Earth's Moon. This would make sense because we know the Megalithic people were great sailors themselves – and especially so in Scotland. A good working knowledge of the Moon would have also offered them valuable information about tides, which in the dangerous waters off the Scottish coast would have been invaluable.

In order to test his theory, Alexander Thom determined to make an extensive study of the stone circles and avenues of the British Isles, though he probably never envisaged that this would become a virtual obsession that would last over 50 years. In any spare time that he had, together with family and friends, Thom meticulously surveyed many hundreds of sites, from Shetland in the north, right down to Brittany in the south. He proved his theories about the Scottish sites and the Moon beyond doubt and also demonstrated that the Sun, planetary bodies other than the Moon, as well as stars and constellations had been of interest to the Megalithic builders.

☩ · ☩ · ☩

In the course of his own research, Alan has probably visited almost as many sites as did Alexander Thom. He began to realize, quite early in his studies, that the sites of individual stones, stone rows and especially stone circles had never been chosen arbitrarily. What almost invariably turned out to be the case was that the planners of these sites had chosen locations with wide vistas on all sides, wherever possible offering a view of distant peaks, spurs, clefts or other natural features that had almost certainly been used as backsights. As an example, if one chooses a particular place to stand in the midst of an area of flat land, and marks the spot, it might be possible to line up oneself with specific astronomical happenings by recourse to something on the distant horizon. One may be able to see the midsummer Sun rise behind a very conspicuous peak, or see the midwinter Sun sink in the west into a natural cleft between two hills. We know, specifically from Thom's own observations, and from work done since, that our ancient ancestors were clever at finding just the right place to put their structures, allowing the maximum number of backsights for a range of astronomical happenings.

So it was that after decades of trudging miles over moorland and bog to see some of the greatest and the most obscure of the Megalithic masterpieces, Alan found himself faced with a very different sort of stone structure – Rosslyn Chapel. At his first visit he noticed that Rosslyn Chapel, with its tall finials, bore a striking resemblance to many of the circles and alignments he had seen in previous years, not so much in terms of the structure itself, but because of where it had been placed on the landscape. We were both well aware that many of the greatest cathedrals, especially in parts of France, had significant astronomical components to their planning and design, and we wondered if the same might be true of this much humbler building in southern Scotland.

As a result, we began to look at Rosslyn Chapel in a way that nobody seems to have done for maybe more than two centuries – not so much as a religious building but as an astronomical observatory, a natural seasonal clock. Anyone who walks around the Chapel at ground level could be forgiven for missing one of the most important facts regarding its placement – after all, as beautiful as the surrounding countryside might be, most people come to look at the Chapel itself. However, up to a very short time ago the building was covered by a huge canopy, held in place on a sturdy steel frame. It had been put there in order to allow the roof and masonry of the Chapel to dry out, ahead of extensive restoration. In truth, the whole thing was ugly, but it was necessary and it served an additional valuable purpose. Those planning the canopy had thoughtfully included a walkway, which went around three sides of the building at a significant height above the ground. When standing on the east side of the walkway, the significance of the Chapel's location on the landscape suddenly began to be more apparent.

Rosslyn Chapel was planned and built on the very edge of a deep, steep-sided valley known as Rosslyn Glen. Beyond the glen to the east is open farmland and in the distance significant hills rise, offering exactly the same sort of panorama that is commonplace in the case of Megalithic stone circles.

Although it is not possible to look west from this side of the Chapel (because the structure itself is in the way), the view from the east side takes in all the area of the sky from northeast to northwest in which the Sun, Moon and all the planets of the solar system can rise throughout any part of the year. When one is even slightly above ground level, there is nothing at all, natural or man-made, that obstructs this view of the eastern sky, and what is more, because the hilly distance has many peaks and clefts, there is ample opportunity for astronomical backsights from the Chapel. It did not take us long to realize that one of these backsights, a significant cleft in the hills, was in just the right position to observe one of the major sunrises of each year – in fact, two such sunrises. These occur at the spring equinox, around 21 March each year, and the autumn equinox, which happens around 21 September.

The positioning of this cleft, into which the Sun *must* rise at the time of the equinoxes, might have been a fortuitous accident, except for one important fact. In the case of the Roman Catholic Church, the feast day of St Matthew, for whom the Chapel is dedicated, is on 21 September – the day of the autumn equinox. In other words, anyone standing, even at ground level, at the centre of the eastern end of the Chapel on 21 September at dawn will see the Sun rise in the cleft that quite naturally occurs in the distance. Because the rising Sun moves up and down the eastern horizon throughout the year – moving by a full degree of arc every day during the spring and autumn, it follows that if the Sun *does not* rise in the cleft, the day in question cannot be that of an equinox.[1]

The Changing Calendar

However, there was a problem, and its solving brought us to an understanding of just how much Earl William, Sir Gilbert Haye, or both, actually knew about astronomy. Until comparatively recently Western Europe was locked into a form of calendar that did not remain accurate from year to year. This had come about because of the adoption, in Roman times, of the Julian calendar. It was the Emperor Julius Caesar who originally called for calendar reform in 46 BC, which is why the Julian system is so named. Unfortunately, when it was devised a simple mistake was made in the way it worked. The Julian year was slightly too short. It assessed the Earth year as being 365.25 days in length, whereas the year is closer to being 365.2564 days. It doesn't seem like too much of a mistake, but over centuries it adds up. The whole thing can seem rather complicated, but what it essentially means is that a known astronomical event, for example the midsummer Sunrise, which occurs on 21 June, will gradually 'drift' through the calendar, so that after several centuries it will no longer occur on the same day in the civil calendar.

This was particularly troublesome to the Christian Church, primarily because of its computations for the date of Easter. Unlike other Christian festivals, Easter is not based on the Sun, but rather it is derived from the movements of the Moon. Its position in the calendar varies from year to year, but by the reign of Pope Gregory XIII (1572–85) it was getting almost impossible to fix it accurately without it converging with other festivals. Pope Gregory therefore decided to reform the calendar and to introduce a more accurate system that would always keep the astronomical year and the civil calendar in tune, one with the other.

By the reign of Pope Gregory, not all Christian countries were under the influence or edicts of Rome, and many Western states were Protestant and totally opposed to any pope. Because of this, countries such as Great Britain did not finally adopt what was known as the Gregorian Calendar until 1752. But Pope Gregory did not even suggest the adoption of the new calendar until 1582, which was almost a century after Rosslyn Chapel was created. This means that at the time the Chapel was built, St Matthew's day and the day of the autumn equinox were a good 10 days apart!

As we explained earlier, it was common practice to build new churches in such a way that the eastern end, or altar, faced the part of the eastern horizon at which the Sun would rise on the feast day of whichever saint carried the dedication of the church. In the case of Rosslyn, the saint was St Matthew, and his feast day was 21 September – yet we know from careful observation that the east end of Rosslyn Chapel faces absolutely due east. If those planning the Chapel had simply followed the Julian calendar, the east end of the Chapel would have faced a position several degrees south of east because in the mid 15th century the autumn equinox was not happening on 21 September. Rather, it occurred closer to 15 September in terms of the Sun rising at the due east position.

This can surely mean only one of two things:

1. The Chapel was built to face due east for reasons other than the feast day of its patron, St Matthew.

2. The planners and builders of Rosslyn Chapel were skilled astronomers and understood the Julian calendar and its failings very well. They therefore orientated the Chapel to the part of the horizon it *should* face, irrespective of the incorrect nature of the calendar in the 15th century.

The Rosslyn Library

Either of these reasons could account for the orientation of the Chapel, and, as we will presently see, the feast day of St Matthew was definitely just one of the reasons why the autumn equinox was so important to its builders. We were to eventually discover that all the information they needed to get the orientation right was already in the library of Earl William. Amongst the manuscripts that were given by Lord Thomas Fairfax to the Bodleian library in Oxford are a number of works on astronomy (a majority of this collection of manuscripts were taken from Rosslyn Castle in 1651). Most of these are to be found in what is now known as MS Fairfax 27. This is a work in three parts, which contains a number of different books. They date to the second quarter of the 13th century and may indeed have been compiled for the Sinclair family.

In these volumes we find forms for ecclesiastical and lay letters, a treatise on the accentuation of words in the Bible and part of the Catholic Epistle of St James. Perhaps more interestingly, also included is a work on mathematics by

Alexander de Villa Dei, entitled 'Carmen de Algorismo'. Even more interesting is *Tractatus de Sphaera* by Johannes de Sacro Bosco, an exhaustive account of Ptolemaic astronomy. This same Johannes, who was most probably an Englishman and who lived circa 1195–1256, was also famed for his work on the calendar. He clearly knew that the Julian calendar was wrong. In another work, *De Anni Ratione*, Johannes made it plain that alterations would definitely have to be made, and he even suggested an alternative strategy by leaving one day out of the calendar every 288 years.

Also included in Fairfax 27 are two works by Gerard of Cremona (circa 1114–47). Although born in Cremona, Gerard set out in search of greater challenges than his home could offer and travelled to Toledo. There he began to translate Arab books that had been left behind when the Western forces of Christianity freed Spain from Arab domination in 1085. The two works in Fairfax 27 are *Theorica Planetarum* and *Quadrans Uetus*. The first relates to astronomical theories regarding the planets and the second deals with mathematics. Finally, Fairfax 27 also contains a number of unattributed scientific treatises, together with calendar and astronomical tables that would have been invaluable to Earl William when it came to placing Rosslyn Chapel.

Many of these works, though only available in universities, were considered to be essential reading for those studying astronomy at the time, but the fact that there is such a strong slant towards works concerning the calendar probably tells its own tale as far as the planning of Rosslyn Chapel was concerned. Even by the 15th century, astronomy was not a subject for the fainthearted. It involved some very complex mathematics, and a good understanding of geometry was also necessary. At the same time, one would have had to be careful when talking about some of the material included in Fairfax 27. A full hundred years after Rosslyn Chapel was being built, the Italian astronomer and all-round genius Galileo came within a hair's breadth of losing his life for suggesting publicly that the Earth spins around the Sun! At the time Rosslyn Chapel was being planned and built, the Catholic Church could still easily have hit out at what it considered to be heretics, even in far-off Scotland.

Anyone who fell under the jurisdiction of the Catholic Church during this period, but who had an eye towards science, had to be extremely careful about how they proceeded, particularly when it came to publishing any findings that did not fall in line with Christian dogma and with what the Church authorities considered was the *genuine* cosmology of the Bible. It is true that the 15th century was not as difficult in this regard as the 16th century would prove to be – probably because of the more liberal-minded popes of the period. All the same, Earl William and Sir Gilbert Haye would have known only too well how sensible it was to disguise any scientific endeavour under a veil of religion. As we hope to demonstrate, this is evident time and again when we really begin to take apart the component parts of Rosslyn Chapel.

✠ · ✠ · ✠

Our realization regarding the care with which the Chapel had been placed on the landscape led us to look more closely than we might otherwise have done at the way the building had been designed. In most churches, the great east window is placed at the *extreme* east end of the building. This allows light from the window to cascade in and shine down on the altar and into the side chapels that are a feature of larger churches. Rosslyn Chapel is quite different with this regard. The extreme eastern end of the above-ground component of the Chapel (where the altar now is) extends beyond the great east window, which does not throw light onto the altar but rather into the body of the church, west of the altar rail. This is because the section of the Chapel known as the retrochoir has a much lower roof than the vaulted roof of the Chapel proper. When the walkway was in place, which visitors could access and thereby walk around three sides of the Chapel well above ground level, the walkway itself was higher than the roof of the retrochoir.

The retrochoir has its own vaulted roof, around which is a low stone wall and the pinnacles that distinguish the whole of the Chapel, but which are especially obvious at the far east end. Anyone standing on this roof and looking east would have the great east window directly behind them and would enjoy an uninterrupted view of the sky from south, right through east, to north. In that area of the sky between southeast and southwest especially, the view is across a wide and generally flat expanse, beyond which hills rise, though at a significant distance from the Chapel itself. (Most of the hills are a good five miles or more away.)

Having established in our own minds that the planners of the Chapel had gone to great trouble to orientate the building accurately on the landscape, and that they had also been very selective regarding *where* they chose to put it, relative to Rosslyn Glen and relative to the distant hills, we wondered if it held more astronomical secrets. The only way we would know

Retrochoir

Observatory
platform

East window

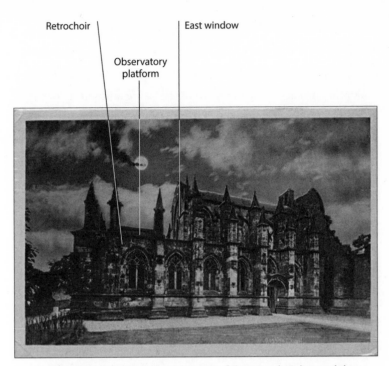

3. Photograph showing the extension of the retrochoir beyond the great east window of Rosslyn Chapel

for sure would be if we could access the roof of the retrochoir directly, which early one quiet spring morning is exactly what we were allowed to do. It was at this time that we discovered the notch in the distant hills that marked spring and autumn equinox sunrise.

When standing on the retrochoir roof, one is surrounded on all sides by the pinnacles. These obscure some parts of the horizon to anyone who is standing immediately at the base of the east window and in the centre of the roof, but it also offers significantly wide spaces from which the horizon to the east can be seen.

An Astronomical Observatory

The location of Rosslyn Chapel is quite significant astronomi-
cally because at 55°51' north of the equator, a geometrical
significance occurs with regard to the rising and setting of the
Sun across the entire year. In order to appreciate this we must
first bear in mind that Rosslyn Chapel was built in an age of
'naked-eye' astronomy. The invention of the telescope was still
150 years away and so everything that was understood about
the sky was a result of unaided astronomy, as indeed was the
case back in the days of the Megalithic builders. Bearing this
in mind, it must have appeared, in pre-telescope days, that
when seen from Rosslyn Chapel, the midwinter Sun rose at 45°
south of east (in other words southeast) and the midsummer
Sun rose at 45° north of east (in other words northeast), thus
forming an exact 90° between the extremes. In reality this is
not quite the case, but the result is so close that it must surely
have been *considered* to be so. This alone would have made
the location deeply interesting to our ancient, star-watch-
ing ancestors and makes one wonder whether rumours that
a Megalithic structure on the site predating Rosslyn Chapel
might not, in fact, be true.[2]

We knew from some of the earliest photographs ever taken,
back in the mid Victorian period, in fact some of the earliest
calotypes taken by Robert Adamson and David O Hill, that the
slightly domed roof of the retrochoir was originally covered
in large, square stone slabs, all of which were the same size.
Standing on different slabs would have altered one's perspective with regard to the pinnacles on the roof and also, therefore,
with their relationship to the horizon. This would have meant
that a wealth of astronomical observations would have been

possible from known positions on the roof (using the pinnacles as foresights and peaks or clefts on the horizon as backsights). Once these had been noted with a record of the slab on which to stand and committed to parchment or to memory, they could be replicated at future times with unerring accuracy.

We hope this information, together with the diagrams included in the plate sections of the book, will fully explain how all of this meant that the east end of Rosslyn Chapel was deliberately and quite obviously created to be an accurate naked-eye astronomical observatory. Since there is no corresponding roof on the west side of the building, it seems that those who created the observatory were primarily concerned with the rising points of the Sun, Moon and planets, though because the retrochoir roof is open on three sides, it would be quite possible to view at least three quarters of the entire sky from the location. (Even at the time of midsummer, when the Sun would have travelled virtually all the way round the Chapel, it would have been possible to see its setting point in the northwest.)

Could all or any of this be a coincidence? It has to be admitted that almost anything could be a coincidence, but in this case there is so much evidence for the deliberate planning and placement of the Chapel that coincidence surely has to be ruled out. To add to the notion that the roof of the retrochoir was regularly accessed, we have the fact that the stone balustrade running between the pinnacles around the retrochoir roof is much lower in one section on the northeast side – as if it was deliberately created this way to allow easy access from the ground by way of a ladder.

There are also narrow elevated pathways under each side of

the lower roofline. These run along the length of the building, under the flying buttresses, from the retrochoir roof and at the same height. They extend along the full north and south sides of the Chapel, allowing an uninterrupted view of the horizon to all points of the compass, except the extreme west end. The western end of the building was substantially altered when a new baptistry was added in the 1880s and we have no way of knowing what it looked like prior to this time. It is therefore possible that even the western end of the Chapel had an access pathway well above ground level, from which astronomical observations could have been made.

There is another architectural anomaly regarding the eastern end of Rosslyn Chapel that might add to the idea that it was a deliberately created astronomical observatory. At ground level there are stone seats built into the eastern wall of the Chapel, facing out across the Glen and to the hills far beyond. These days, there is no appreciable view from these seats because a high stone wall was erected in Victorian times and this obscures the view. However, this wall did not exist when the Chapel was built. The only part of the Chapel beyond this point is the lower Chapel (or crypt), but the roof of this does not rise higher than the general ground level and would not have obstructed the view from these stone seats. We searched diligently but we could find no other example in which seats of this sort were incorporated into the fabric of a church building. Although the degree of accuracy achievable from the retrochoir roof, with its regular, square stone slabs could not have been achieved at ground level, the view of the eastern horizon from the seats would still have been stunning in the days before light pollution was a problem.

4. The roof path on the southern side

Further proof that the *absolute* placement of the Chapel with regard to the points of the compass had been considered crucial from its inception became evident as a result of what seemed at first to be little more than a legend. John has a cousin, Nancy Bruce, whose association with the Chapel goes right back to her own childhood. This connection continued

5. Seats at east end of Chapel

until the present because she ultimately became one of the guides at the Chapel. We were talking to her one day, early in our research about the Chapel's connection with St Matthew, and she related a story we had not heard before. She told us that on St Matthew's day each year, a red light was said to shine into the Chapel from the east end, illuminating the interior of the building. For a while we were puzzled by this story, but when we traced the red light, it introduced us to yet another facet of this remarkable building that contributes to making Rosslyn Chapel an undisputed gem and also a place of carefully contrived magic.

CHAPTER SEVEN

The Blood-Red Light

I t is not unusual to see astronomical and astrological iconography in churches, even very old ones, and it can
often be viewed in prime positions. England's premier
cathedral at Canterbury, for example, has a set of very old, large
roundels depicting the signs of the zodiac on the floor near the
tomb of King Henry IV and the Trinity Chapel. Not far from
Canterbury, on the Romney Marshes in Kent, is the parish
church of St Augustine in the village of Brooklands. This has
an extremely ancient lead font, around which all the signs of
the zodiac are to be seen, together with a list of suggested jobs
to be undertaken at the relevant time of year. Also in the south
of England is Copford Church, described as one of the most
beautiful of England's parish churches. In the 19th century, a
number of old wall paintings were discovered in the church.
These had been painted over in Tudor times or perhaps after
the English Civil War. One of them depicts a complete zodiac,
together with a Sun and Moon. These are on the underside of
the chancel arch, where absolutely no attempt had been made

to hide them from the congregation. These may date from the 15th century, but nobody is certain.

Essex is home to the magnificent Waltham Abbey. There are some beautiful ceiling paintings in the church itself and amongst them are depicted all the zodiacal signs. Zodiac symbols can also be seen in the church of St Mary in Beverley, East Yorkshire, and there are no doubt dozens of other examples, sometimes lost or still covered as wall and ceiling paintings, or hiding away beneath the small ledges known as misericords that are to be found in the choirs of hundreds of parish churches the length and breadth of the British Isles.

All of this serves to demonstrate that there was no actual taboo involved in the use of astronomical and astrological iconography in the Church, especially prior to the 16th century. It was only slightly later, probably partly because the Catholic Church was under attack from the embryonic rise of science and Protestantism, that those creating churches had to be rather more circumspect regarding what they put on display for their parishioners. After all, the signs of the zodiac invariably served to illustrate the passing year, which was of great importance in both a religious and a civil sense. The seasonal round ruled the lives of everyone back in the days when farming was the norm, and even townspeople were tied to the calendar in terms of what was available to eat – or not. However, most of the fascination for astronomy in ecclesiastical circles in medieval times could be explained away (when explanations may have been necessary) in terms of the perpetual search for Easter, which we mentioned in the previous chapter. Many of the important Christian festivals were tied to the solar calendar. This applied particularly to Christmas, from which many other feast days were calculated. But the other important Christian cornerstone of the year, and arguably the most significant, had to be Easter, another festival around which much of the Church year pivoted.

All the same, it is obvious in some cases that a fascination for the passing year went much further than an attempt to tie down the elusive date of Easter. There are occasions when those planning churches and cathedrals were locking into something far more pagan than the understandable use of astronomy for liturgical purposes. A good case in question appears in the wonderful cathedral of Chartres, in France. This incredible building, erected between 1193 and 1250, is particularly worth a mention because we hope to show that in some ways it has much in common with Rosslyn Chapel. For the moment we will content ourselves with pointing out its sizeable number of zodiacs and also one of its stained-glass windows, which portrays scenes in the life of a fairly obscure saint by the name of Apollinaris.

The window in question was very carefully created. On just one small area it contains a piece of absolutely clear glass amidst the bright colours surrounding it. This was deliberately placed within the window to serve a very specific function. The part of the window in question portrays the god Apollo, who was a solar deity. On the day of the summer solstice, the light of the Sun comes streaming in through this single piece of plain glass and strikes a point on the floor of the cathedral. There is nothing accidental about this because a handmade nail was driven into the floor many centuries ago at the point where the small pool of light is to be seen. Whoever devised this neat little yearly trick must have gone to great trouble to arrange things this way – especially when one considers that the subject matter of the window in question relates directly to a pagan god of the Sun. Although the context of St Apollinaris confirms a deeply religious context, the pagan overtones tell a different story.

Also in France is a later church, that of Saint-Sulpice in the city of Paris. Saint-Sulpice is the second largest church in Paris after Notre Dame, and although there has been a church on the site since the 13th century, the present building dates mostly from as recently as the 18th century. Saint-Sulpice had the honour of happening to stand on the prime meridian of France, which was established in the 18th century by the French Academy of Science. In order to commemorate the fact, a priest of the time, Jean-Baptiste Languet de Gergy, decided to add a gnomon inside the church building – claiming that its addition would assist in calendar rectification and therefore aid that seemingly impossible task of fixing the true date of Easter. This cannot have been the real reason because by this date the Gregorian calendar had been accepted universally and there was no doubt about when Easter should be.

Be that as it may, the learned cleric had his gnomon erected and also arranged for a lens to be set up in one of the windows in the south transept of the church, which would allow light to pass down the metal line on the floor marking the prime meridian and illuminate an obelisk of stone beyond, which represents the gnomon. This only happens on the day of the winter solstice. However, it was also arranged that the ray of light should shine into the church on the days of the spring and autumn equinoxes, this time illuminating an oval copper plate, set into the floor very close to the altar.

None of this came into being until 1743, by which time astronomy was moving on in leaps and bounds, but together with the earlier examples it serves to illustrate the fact that the 'corners of the year' as they are known, ie the solstices and the equinoxes, have always fascinated people – who sought in many ways to track them and to give evidence of the days on which they occurred. There is nothing remotely new about this as far as the British Isles in concerned. The standing stone circle of Stonehenge, which dates from around 3000 BC to 2000 BC, had alignments specifically for the solstices and no doubt the equinoxes, too. Even burial chambers such as Maes Howe in Scotland and Newgrange in Ireland, which were roughly contemporary but probably slightly earlier than Stonehenge, were deliberately created so that the light of the summer or winter solstice would shine down their entry tunnels and into the burial chamber beyond.

It might be suggested that the vast majority of standing stone circles and alignments that existed, and often still exist across the British Isles, were created *specifically* to track the year, an obsession that seems to have been just as relevant before Christianity as it turned out to be after the new religion had gained sway in Europe. In other words, things never altered – even if the sort of structure used to plot and track the changing face of the sky across the year altered significantly.

✢ · ✢ · ✢

Despite the fact that astronomical information and iconography can be found in many humble churches, and especially in Western Europe's magnificent cathedrals, there can surely be no better example than that found at Rosslyn Chapel. Upon entering the building and looking up, there is no doubt from the outset that cosmology was fully intended to lie at the heart of the construction of the building. The barrel vault of the main church roof is positively covered with stars. There are so many, interspersed with a Sun and a Moon, as well as with flowers and other symbols, that one is forced to wonder whether some particular star pattern is intended (in other words, relating to a view of the changing sky fixed for one specific historical date). If this is the case, we have not yet been able to work out what that date may have been.

Further proof of the importance of astronomy to Rosslyn Chapel is to be found on the outside of the building, where over one southern-facing window, depictions of all the signs of the zodiac from Leo to Capricorn are to be seen. There are probably other zodiac carvings outside the Chapel but the stonework in this harsh and unremitting climate has suffered significantly where it has been exposed to the fierce northern blasts, and much of it is difficult or impossible to make out.

Back inside the Chapel, each upper corner has the depiction of a male head, which have always been said to be St Matthew, St Mark, St Luke and St John – the four Evangelists. Although these are biblical characters, and also recognized as being the writers of the New Testament Gospels, their presence in the corners of the building can also tell its own astronomical tale. This is because the four Gospel writers have always been associated with the Old Testament descriptions of the four creatures that surrounded the throne of God (and which also appear in the Book of Revelation). These were said to be an angel for St Matthew, a winged lion for St Mark, a winged bull for St Luke and an eagle for St John. These, in turn, have been connected to astronomy and astrology. (Actually, there may be a direct connection between Jesus' 12 disciples and the 12 signs of the zodiac that originated very early in the development of Christianity.)

Probably for reasons of iconography, St Mark was supposed to represent the zodiac sign of Leo; St Luke, as the bull, represents the zodiac sign of Taurus; St John the Evangelist, as an eagle, represents Scorpio, which often used to be called Aquilla the eagle – and St Matthew therefore represented the zodiac sign of Aquarius. All of these signs have something in common. In terms of the zodiac they stand three signs apart and are known as the 'fixed' signs of the zodiac.

Unlike churches such as Chartres and Saint-Sulpice, Rosslyn Chapel was not built to reflect the solstices of the year but rather the equinoxes. It did not, therefore, unduly surprise us to learn that, in tradition at least, provision had been made to celebrate the two equinox days *inside* the Church, as had been arranged for the solstices at Chartres and Saint-Sulpice.

Since Rosslyn Chapel is orientated to the points of the compass, and since the equinoxes can only take place with the Sun rising due east, provision for the Sun shining directly into the Chapel interior would have to have been made at the eastern end. But how could this be the case? The biggest window in the Chapel is the great east window, which covers a huge area, from just above the entrance to the retrochoir to almost the top point of the building. It stands to reason that whenever light shines from the east, it will flood into the Chapel on any day of the year. Thus, we knew that the celebration of the equinoxes, if it took place at all, had to be marked in some specific way.

An Amazing Discovery

It was at this point that we began to study the great east window carefully, which at the time was made easier for us because of the walkway that ran around the outside of the building on the south, east and north sides, well above ground level. On the east side this gave a panoramic view of the east window from the exterior of the building that would not have been possible unless the walkway was in place. As a result we soon found what we were looking for.

In the top part of the point of the east window is a small section that looks like simple ornamentation. There are two small stone arms running down from the inner point of the arch, covering what looks, from a distance, like a circular hole through the stone window frame. When viewed close up, this is not a circle at all but rather a pentagonal shape. The detail surrounding this pentagonal hole copies the detail to be found in the circular part of the window below, so does not look out of place and would not even be recognized as anything special unless viewed very close up, or through a strong lens, such as that of a high-powered camera. From ground level, as it is commonly seen, it can barely be noticed at all.

It was immediately obvious to us, thanks to the advanced photographic equipment that John was able to provide, that this five-sided opening was lined with some sort of metal. Strangely, whatever this metal actually is, it has not oxidized or even darkened in colour, despite the fact that it must have been in place for a very long period of time.

We were certain that this strange little feature must have something to do with the occurrence of the 'special light' inside the Chapel on St Matthew's Day, but we were somewhat

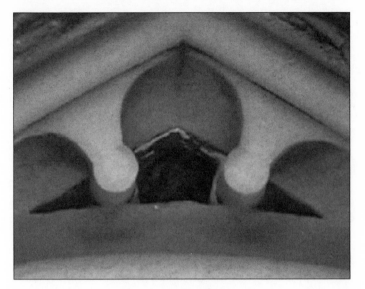

6. Rosslyn light box

hampered by two facts. First of all, St Matthew's Day, and therefore the day of the autumn equinox, was some months away, and secondly, the presence of the temporary canopy over the Chapel would prevent light from falling onto this part of the window in any case. It seemed the only way forward was to create our own equinox, and with the aid of a very high-powered torch and a telescopic rod, this is exactly what we did.

We fastened the torch to the telescopic rod. John took this up onto the walkway and Alan retreated to the western end of the Chapel, up in the Victorian organ loft, to see what, if anything, would happen. Down below in the Chapel, a tour was taking place and people were attending to the guide talking in the retrochoir, so they did not witness what Alan and his wife Kate saw from the organ loft. Alan was communicating with John via a walkie-talkie, but as it turned out this wasn't necessary. As soon as John moved the torch level with the opening at the top of the window on the outside of the building, a very bright, blood-red light appeared at the point of the window inside the Chapel. Both Alan and Kate let out a gasp of wonder, which they immediately stifled so as not to disturb the visitors below. We then changed places so that John could see the effect for himself.

Going back to the walkway, we looked again at what we had already come to call the light box. It was clearly not simply a hole through the masonry of the window top. When the torch was shone into the opening, much of the beam was reflected straight back and became a blazing light, which was quite blinding, even in the full light of day. It was as if the light was reflecting off a high-powered mirror, though in reality what was inside the hole seemed to be faceted because the returning light came out at all angles. However, from the outside of the building there was no trace of red light – it was pure white.

The light box is situated at the highest point of the east window, very close to the roof of the Chapel. Even with the walkway in place it was not possible to get close to it, except by the use of telephoto-lens photography. We were therefore unable to examine the metal-lined hole directly. Somewhere within it there has to be a red filter, which turns the bright light falling into the shaft into the blood-red glow that appears in the Chapel. When viewed through a high-powered telephoto lens, it becomes obvious that this red filter has either become misplaced or is very slightly damaged, because to one side of the red light, a little white light spills through, though bearing in mind how long this device has probably been in place, this is not surprising.

Precisely how the device works and what its true composition might be remains unknown. What *is* certain is that the light box cannot have come to occupy its present position or serve its function by chance. It was carefully designed and deliberately created to do what it does.

☩ · ☩ · ☩

It is worth a slight diversion at this point to try and understand when the light box came into existence. We do know that the design of the east window as we see it today is not the same as the window that was first placed in the east end of the Chapel. This window was redesigned in the 1860s, as a memorial to the memory of the sister of the then Earl of Rosslyn. In terms of its tracery, the present window is substantially different, and we know this to be the case because in the very earliest days of photography, two local men, whose names were David Hill and Robert Adamson, formed a partnership that lasted four years, between 1843 and 1847. Hill and Adamson were based in Edinburgh, but they took pictures known as calotypes, many of which survive. Some of these were taken at Rosslyn Chapel, most likely around 1845, and they represent an invaluable source of evidence as to the state of the Chapel at that time.

One of the Hill and Adamson photographs was taken from the roof of the retrochoir, and it shows the glassless east window, with a man sitting on the sill and facing outwards.

The infuriating fact about these pictures is that they do not show enough detail within the point of the arch to say with any certainty whether or not the light box existed in the original window of the newly built chapel.

There are two possibilities. Either the light box was envisaged and created when the Chapel was built in the second half of the 15th century, or it was designed and created sometime shortly after 1862 for James Alexander Erskine-Sinclair, third Earl of Rosslyn, at which time the east window was remodelled. Although the two periods are four centuries apart, in a way it is immaterial which of the Sinclair dynasty envisaged creating this wonderful feature. Its presence bears testimony to the care and knowledge that went into designing and orientating the Chapel in the first place, and it complements the naked-eye observatory that exists immediately below it on the roof of the retrochoir – a feature of the building that definitely *does* date back to the 15th century.

We were also forced to ask ourselves if the Rosslyn Chapel light box (whether it was created in the 15th century or the 19th century) had been designed specifically *just* to denote equinox days. It does this job admirably. Now that the walkway and canopy have been removed from the Chapel, it is once again possible for the rays of the rising Sun to strike the uppermost part of the window, where the light box is situated. John has been able to view the result on a clear morning at the time of the autumn equinox and reported the light glowing red and obvious inside the Chapel.

Whatever the make-up of the interior of the light box may be, there is no doubt that it was created not simply to allow light to pass through it, and to alter that light from white to red, but to amplify the light and to capture it at a particular angle relative to the window. The light box would certainly respond to the Moon if it was in the right position in the sky, and of course the effect inside the Chapel would be that much

7. Early 19th-century photograph of the ruined east window of
Rosslyn Chapel with close-up detail

greater when the building was in darkness. But the same would be true regarding the light created by the third brightest object that appears in our night skies – the planet Venus.

Because of the peculiarities of its orbit and the way it is seen from the Earth, Venus can only ever illuminate the light box when it rises as a bright morning star, before the Sun rises. Even then, the event would have to take place at a specific part of the year, either around the spring equinox or the autumn equinox. The effect would be even more stunning if the innermost planet of the solar system, Mercury, was also to be involved. In other words, if Mercury and Venus were rising together, ahead of the Sun, at either spring or autumn equinox, and if the sky was clear, the light box seen from inside the Chapel would glow steady and red and would look stunning within the body of the Chapel, where no other light would be penetrating at the time.

The Shekinah

The involvement of Mercury in this scenario would mean that the event could only take place for a very short period immediately before the Sun itself began to rise. This is because Mercury has an orbit that stays close to the Sun. From an earthbound perspective Mercury can only be seen well in the east immediately before sunrise.

This event, the coming together of Venus and Mercury in what is known as a close conjunction, immediately before dawn, is quite rare. It has been associated, especially by the writers Christopher Knight and Robert Lomas,[1] with something that was of supreme importance to the early Jewish community. To them, the event was known as a Shekinah.

1 (top) View of Rosslyn Chapel in the 1860s, taken from below, in Rosslyn Glen

2 (above) Depiction of the angel who regularly accompanies St Matthew on Medieval paintings and sculptures; note the open book

3 (right) The Apprentice Pillar or Prince's Pillar is the most southerly of three ornate pillars placed between the body of the Chapel and the retrochoir. It supports Freemasonic legend about a murdered apprentice, but, more importantly, relates to the story of St Matthew and his visit to the city of Myrna.

4 (above) The tetrahedron of Gordian knots at the top of the middle of the Chapel's three ornate pillars

5 (below) A view of the interior of Rosslyn Chapel, looking east from the body of the Chapel into the retrochoir or Lady Chapel

6 (below right) One of the Chapel's pinnacles on the roofline above the northeastern end of the Chapel is deliberately created as a beehive. Even within living memory, honey from this hive dripped through a carefully created channel into the Chapel and onto the altar below.

7 (right) A depiction of Enea Piccolomini, Pope Pius II, surrounded by the Scottish nobility and prior to his papacy

8 (below) The view of the hills from the east end of Rosslyn Chapel, clearly showing the 'notch' in the hills that marks equinox sunrise

9 (top left) The observatory platform that is the roof of the retrochoir below; in this case showing north and northeast

10 (left) A view of the lower roofline of Rosslyn Chapel demonstrating how the horizon is split into equal sections when viewed from the building's walkways

11 (bottom) The astronomical observatory as seen from the ground on the south side of the building

12 (right) Early photograph of the eastern end of the Chapel, showing the stone seats at ground level

13 (below) Rosslyn Chapel ceiling with its complexity of stars

14 (above) A demonstration of what happens when light is shone into the light box from outside the building, showing the reflective glass contents of the tube

15 (below) An extreme close-up of the light box from the interior of the Chapel when external light shines directly into it. The blood-red light can clearly be seen.

16 (right) The Green Man is an important character in British folklore. There are many representations of Green Men at Rosslyn Chapel.

17 (below) This example of a carved Green Man, of which there is a multitude inside and outside Rosslyn Chapel, occupies the back of a statue niche, high up on the northern side of the exterior of the building. It was rediscovered during recent renovations and cannot be seen from ground level, so was invisible to anyone for well over 500 years.

18 (top) Detail of the carving of King Darius from the east end of the Chapel

19 (above) A representation of the Knights Templar emblem, the Agnus Dei, carved into a pillar top at Rosslyn Chapel

20 (right) This statue, believed to be St Matthew, is presently at Rosslyn Castle but most probably came from the Chapel originally

Knight and Lomas pointed out that the appearance of the Shekinah was associated particularly in the Old Testament of the Bible with kingship, and since kingship amongst the early Hebrews lasted for a prescribed period of time, it seemed likely that the Shekinah was a predictable, repeatable happening. This association of Mercury and Venus, in the right place on the horizon and meeting as a full conjunction (in other words creating not two lights but one light), is a 40-year cycle. Alan assisted Christopher Knight and Robert Lomas regarding the astronomical component of their book *Uriel's Machine* and spent weeks tracking down the occurrence of the Shekinah as a manifestation of Mercury/Venus conjunctions, throughout prehistory.

The Shekinah was an especially important event to the Hebrews, and it was usually associated with the Holy of Holies of the Temple of Solomon in Jerusalem. Like Rosslyn Chapel, Solomon's Temple faced east, across falling ground and with nothing at the time to obscure the eastern horizon. In the Holy of Holies, which was curtained off from the rest of the Temple and was approachable only by certain high priests, stood the Ark of the Covenant, a gold-covered wooden box that originally contained the laws of the Hebrews as prescribed by God. The Hebrews also believed that God Himself existed within the Ark. Judaism, like all religions, developed from a host of previous beliefs, brought together around the time the Hebrews conquered and settled in the Near East, where they chose Jerusalem as their capital city.

Arks such as the one described in the Old Testament of the Bible were not unique to the Hebrews and they most probably got the idea during the time they had stayed as a client tribe in Egypt. On top of the lid of the Ark were two gold angels. Their outstretched and curved wings came together to form a gap just above the Ark, and it seems likely that the Ark stood in front of an aperture in the wall of the Temple, through which the eastern horizon was visible. When the Shekinah appeared (and the priests knew from past experience and from their knowledge of astronomy when this would occur), the combined light of Mercury and Venus rose above the horizon (which from the perspective of those inside the Holy of Holies was level with the lid of the Ark) and the single light appeared to stand between the outstretched and curved wings of the angels. As the Sun began to rise towards the horizon, the combined light of Mercury and Venus, which is extremely bright in the predawn glow of the Sun, turned blood red, before disappearing into the light of the risen Sun.

It must have looked truly spectacular, as indeed it still does on those relatively rare occasions when circumstances allow it to take place. To the Hebrews, the Shekinah that was most potent occurred in the month of the year that corresponds to our September (at the time of the autumn equinox).

The Shekinah, because of the gender of the word, has always been considered a 'feminine' concept, and it may once have been thought that the presence of the Shekinah in close proximity to the Ark represented a communion between the male and female components of Godhead.

✠ · ✠ · ✠

This is all very interesting, but what could it have to do with Rosslyn Chapel, which after all is supposed to be a Christian church and not a Hebrew Temple? Strangely, quite a few people have suggested that Rosslyn Chapel has far more in common with a typical temple than it does with the average church, and the writers Christopher Knight and Robert Lomas in their book, *The Hiram Key*, suggested that Rosslyn Chapel was a deliberately created version of what people in the 15th century thought Solomon's Temple may well have looked like.[2]

Also of significant interest is the fact that the middle of the three ornate pillars that stand to the east of the Chapel, immediately in front of the retrochoir, used to be known as the Shekinah Pillar. By Victorian times, in other words by the time the east window was recreated, the pillars were known by their Freemasonic names, which were the Apprentice Pillar, the Journeyman Pillar and the Master's Pillar. Prior to this, probably ever since the Chapel was created, they were known as the Earl's Pillar, the Shekinah Pillar and the Prince's Pillar.

The Shekinah Pillar stands directly below the middle of the east window, in the very centre of the Chapel, directly in line with the light that emanates from the light box above. Of even more interest, the Shekinah Pillar contains carvings, close to its top, of ornate and exquisitely executed interlaced pentagonal stars. There is a strong connection between the Shekinah and five-pointed stars because the pentangle is the most common pictorial representation of the planet Venus. This is not simply because the star shape itself represents Venus in a pictorial sense, but relates directly to the relationship between Venus and our own Earth.

Earth and Venus are locked into orbits that are mathematically closely related. Venus takes 224.7 days to orbit the Sun, but because the Earth is also travelling in its own orbit, the view we get of Venus does not represent the true orbital period of the planet. To us, using naked-eye observation, Venus appears to take 584 days to pass around the sky, which means there is an 8:5 relationship between the orbit of the Earth, at 365 days, and the perceived orbit of Venus at 584 days. (For every 8 Earth years, 5 Venus years appear to take place.) The result is that the reoccurring patterns formed by Venus across the sky during a 40-year period seem to trace out a perfect five-pointed star.

Whoever decided to call the middle decorated pillar in Rosslyn Chapel the Shekinah Pillar was associating it with elements of Hebrew mythology that are also related to the mythologies of other peoples with whom the Hebrews mixed, fought, intermarried and coexisted in the area of Palestine. In its feminine persona, the Shekinah is closely related to major female deities that predominated in this part of the world, and which were also significant to the Hebrews prior to the absolute adoption of monotheistic male-centred religion. The goddess of the region had many names, but amongst them were Astarte, Inanna, Ashtoreth, Lilith and even Isis. In Palestine, her worship often involved the creation and adoration of pillars, which represented the goddess. The same was true for the Minoans on the Island of Crete, which is not far from the Mediterranean shore of Palestine and which may have heavily affected the cultures there.[3]

The Goddess and the Kabbalah

There are accounts in the Old Testament of the Bible in which the sacred sites of Ashtoreth, with their pillars, were sought out and destroyed, though the Bible makes it clear that even the revered King Solomon (purportedly king from 970 BC to 931 BC) was a worshipper of Ashtoreth. Given that in the most ancient traditions, the Shekinah was synonymous with this great goddess of the Eastern Mediterranean, she too would have been worshipped in the form of a pillar. In so many cases the name 'Shekinah' is almost certainly merely an alternative for Ashtoreth or Ashoret.

Most of the stories associating the Shekinah with the ancient goddess and with sacred pillars, trees or poles come not from the Bible but from the Kabbalah. The Kabbalah is a repository of mystical Jewish writings that began to emerge in Europe after the 11th century, eventually becoming popular with non-Jewish scholars and thinkers – particularly by the 16th century. In one of the stories from the Kabbalah, Lilith, who was supposed to be the first wife of Adam, was turned into a Shekinah Pillar. This story also makes mention of the planet Venus and the five-pointed star that has always represented the planet.

A particular branch of Kabbalism was Lurianic Kabbalism, named after Isaac Luria, who was born in Jerusalem in 1534. Despite the name, this branch of Kabbalism is far older than the 16th century. Lurianic Kabbalists referred to the male component of God as 'the Holy Blessed One' and saw Him as being distinct and yet one with the Shekinah. They believed that these two forces did not always agree, because each expressed the message of Godhead in a different way. As a result, there was a period during each year when the Holy Blessed One and the Shekinah separated for a while. This separation took place a few days before the start of the Jewish New Year celebrations. The Holy Blessed One and the Shekinah were said to reunite as the New Year commenced, in the month of Tishri. The Jewish

New Year commenced at the time of the autumn equinox, in the month we now call September! The solar illumination of the light box at Rosslyn Chapel in September therefore marks St Matthew's day, but also the start of the Jewish New Year. The symbolism of the red light appearing over the east window at this time would not have been lost on Kabbalists, especially those of the Lurianic variety. Red was the colour associated with the Shekinah.

There are significant implications here because we know that Earl William Sinclair was a collector of books on a grand scale. Some of the works that still survive, particularly those in the Bodleian Library in Oxford, deal specifically with alchemy, which was very popular throughout Europe and beyond during medieval times and later. The main aims of alchemy were to transmute base metals such as lead into gold, and also to create something referred to as the 'philosopher's stone', which, in turn, could supposedly offer any individual immortality. Alchemy sounds laughable these days, but it should not be forgotten that many of the experiments that founded the beginning of real science had been made possible because of alchemy. If anyone doubts this, they should perhaps study the life of Sir Isaac Newton, often said to be the father of science. During his life Newton spent far more time experimenting with alchemy than he ever did on the subjects for which he is best known today.

Like many alchemists, Isaac Newton was also deeply interested in the Kabbalah and was especially fascinated by King Solomon's Temple and its supposed proportions. Newton was born nearly 200 years after Rosslyn Chapel was commenced, but books about both alchemy and the Kabbalah were readily available in the 15th century, as the remnants of Earl William Sinclair's library testify.

✠ · ✠ · ✠

We have to ask ourselves whether or not those who planned Rosslyn Chapel were really *only* the devout Christians that their obsession with St Matthew seems to suggest. If this was the case, what was their interest in the Shekinah? Whatever that interest turns out to have been, it was evident from the moment the Chapel was first envisaged. The light box may have been created in either the 15th or the 19th century, but the existence of the Shekinah Pillar is contemporary with the creation of the building. Whilst the light box would *recreate* the mystical Shekinah each time Venus rose due east as a morning star, the Shekinah Pillar was ever-present, occupying that all-important place, below the centre of the east window.

It was in 1446 that the building of the Chapel was sanctioned by Rome, and by 1456, the township created by Earl William, and now known as Roslin, had received its charters from the Scottish Crown. Clearly, the Chapel could not be commenced until the intended workers had somewhere to live, so we were always of the opinion that 1456 was the most likely time for the project to be commenced. Imagine our surprise, then, when we took a look at 21 September 1456 and discovered that on that morning, 1 hour and 10 minutes before dawn, Mercury and Venus rose together over the eastern horizon. This was a near perfect conjunction – in fact, a Shekinah – and it occurred on St Matthew's day in the very year that the building of Rosslyn Chapel commenced. If the sky were clear, and we have no way of knowing whether it was, this event could have been seen from the very spot where the Chapel would stand – a good omen and hardly likely to have been a coincidence. It appears that Earl William Sinclair and his able assistant Sir Gilbert Haye not only knew a great deal about astronomy, but were also conversant with the Kabbalah and with alchemy.

✣ · ✣ · ✣

Almost from the very start of our combined research into Rosslyn Chapel we have described it as being like the many skins of an onion – composed not of one cohesive intention or reality but many. It was conceived and created at a pivotal point in European history. The Chapel reflects the most forward-looking ideas of its day, as well as being a legacy of the ancient past, and anyone wishing to truly understand its complexities also has to realize that it is much more than merely a partly finished late Gothic masterpiece.

CHAPTER EIGHT

Peeling Back the Layers

A ll the books in the world would not, of themselves, have made either Earl William Sinclair or Sir Gilbert Haye into either stonemasons or sculptors. It stands to reason that it would have taken the best master craftsmen of the period to create such amazing carvings as those at Rosslyn Chapel, which by common consent are as good as anything created across Europe at the time – and in many cases better. Victorians, writing about Rosslyn Chapel, seem to have been of the opinion that these master craftsmen came from far away – most likely France and Italy. It was always supposed that the building of the township of Roslin, contemporary with the creation of the Chapel, was to house these foreign workers but in reality these are just suggestions and there isn't a scrap of proof that anyone was brought from outside Scotland to work on the Chapel.

Perhaps these writers can be forgiven for assuming that Scotland could not have supplied the artistry that went into Rosslyn Chapel. In the Victorian period, Scotland was still suffering, in some ways, from the opinions of its southern neighbour England. Scotland was much beloved of Queen Victoria and her husband Prince Albert, who spent a protracted part of each year north of the border. Not only did Victoria and Albert (and later especially Victoria, as a widow) find peace and solace amidst the stunning countryside to which they took themselves on a regular basis, to a certain extent they began to *re-create* Scotland in their own image, in particular with the help of Scottish romantic novelist Sir Walter Scott.

Victorian England, and in particular the cities, was a place of dark satanic mills, coal mines, steel works, overcrowded streets, short life expectancy and social deprivation. The industrialization that was taking place took little account of the needs of a rapidly growing population. In London, black, foul-smelling smog often swirled around dirty streets, crowding in on the River Thames that was so filthy politicians in the Palace of Westminster could not tolerate the stink, especially in the summer. Victoria and Albert spent much of the year in Buckingham Palace, in the very centre of London, and though they may have been surrounded by luxury at an immediate level, they were certainly not immune to the sights, sounds and odour of London itself. How wonderful therefore to be able to pack up and travel for several weeks each year to a place that was clean and quiet, quaint and picture-perfect.

Scotland too had its industry and its crowded cities, but not in the part of the country that Victoria and her entourage chose to spend their holidays. It was a little like any one of us choosing to take our vacation at some tiny fishing village in Portugal or at a remote farmhouse in the French Dordogne. What the Royal family created at Balmoral in particular was a fantasy Scotland, of the sort still to be seen on tins of Highland shortbread. It was a world of tartan shawls and kilts, deer hunting and grouse shooting, highland dancing and lone pipers on the battlements – and about as far from the reality of Scotland as it was possible to get!

What was good enough for the Queen was more than good enough for court followers, and even the English middle classes who could afford the fare. As a result, Scotland was 'rebranded', and to some extent it is still being sold in the same package to this day. To the well-heeled Victorian English, Scotland was cute, extremely picturesque, filled with loyal gillies, beautiful red-haired girls and single malt whisky, but it would never have been considered 100 per cent civilized because that was the last thing the visitors wanted. They thought of it as the territory of the Celtic 'noble savage' and that was the way they liked it.

The truth is that although Scotland has never enjoyed the wealth of England, it was closely associated with what was considered to be the most cultured country in Europe. Its relationship with France and its trading ties to other states in Europe offered an outward-looking attitude. Meanwhile, its broadly egalitarian tendencies brought education to even the lowliest potential student. Scotland had no less than five universities at a time when other European states had none, and when England had only two, Oxford and Cambridge. With only a barrel of salt herring and a sack of oatmeal to pay his way, any weaver's son or crofter's child with a good report from the 'dominie' of his local community could avail himself of the education on offer – and many did.

The Tironensian Order

As we have seen, Scotland was certainly awake to what was going on in the more southern, sunnier areas of Europe as the Renaissance began to gain pace, and with so many potential foreign contacts on offer it is probably fair to suggest that Earl William could have procured sculptors and stonemasons from Italy or France in order to create his masterpiece. On the other hand, why should he have done so when some of the finest craftsmen in the world were right on his doorstep?

Earl William had land all over Scotland. Some of his holdings were further west than Rosslyn, and one township that fell under his sway was the ancient settlement of Kilwinning, in north Ayrshire. By the 15th century, it was a thriving community, industrious and prosperous, but it owed its existence to the 'cells' or 'kills' of very early Christian monks who settled in the area. One of these was St Winin – hence the name Kilwinning.

With an early air of sanctity it is not surprising that Kilwinning became the site of several successive monasteries, probably dating back to the 8th century or earlier, though the most recent abbey was commenced as early as 1140.

The monks who toiled to build Kilwinning Abbey, the ruins of which are still to be seen today, were no strangers to Scotland, though they came originally from France. These were the monks of Tiron, one of the largest of the reformed Benedictine orders of the 12th century. The Tironensian order was incredibly successful, especially in Scotland, and yet as far as history is concerned they have been all but forgotten. Theirs is a fascinating story, and their efforts undoubtedly had a part to play in the development of the world we live in today. Part of the reason they are not better remembered is that they have been historically eclipsed by their much more famous cousins, the Cistercians. However, what they were famed for, which was never the case with the Cistercians, was their incredible building skills.

The Tironensian monks owed their existence to their founder, Bernard of Tiron, who was born around 1050 near Abbeville, in the former province of Ponthieu in northern France. Bernard chose a monastic life, or more probably had it chosen for him, and he ended up in a Benedictine abbey close to his home. It didn't take long for Bernard to become disillusioned with the Benedictine rule. The order had been founded centuries earlier, and though St Benedict, as founder, had always intended that its monks should live an impoverished life of work and prayer, things had changed dramatically.

Young Bernard longed for a more devout life and so, for many years, he became a recluse and a hermit. His basic problem was that he did not agree with the way Rome ran the Church and, in particular, did not care for the way bishops and cardinals interfered with monastic houses. Bernard spent many years in Brittany, which at the time was not part of the kingdom of France; neither was Christianity in Brittany the same as it was in other parts of mainland Europe. Brittany, and especially its abbeys, followed a tradition that was Scottish and Irish in origin. This peculiar form of Christianity was known as Culdean and is recognized by many as *being* the Celtic Church. It was, for centuries, an irritating thorn in the side of the Roman Catholic Church.

Eventually, in 1105, Bernard founded the community of Tiron, which is how he acquired the second part of his name –

he is referred to as Bernard of Tiron or Thiron. The Tironensian order was, from the outset, dedicated to a life of unremitting work and prayer. Its rules were harsh and the living conditions of its monks were far from easy. Bernard had a vision, and it was a slightly different vision from that of his near contemporary and protector, another Bernard, this time Bernard of Clairvaux. Bernard of Clairvaux was the spiritual and practical creator of the Cistercian order of monks, even though he had not actually founded the order; it sang his song, and was also dedicated to a hard and abstemious life. However, there were quite significant differences between the Tironensian monks and those of the Cistercian order, which predominantly had to do with the way they were structured and their ultimate intentions.

The Cistercians were hard workers, principally agriculturists, but much of the manual work that saw them positively exploding across the landscape of Europe and beyond in the 12th and 13th centuries was undertaken by a form of 'under-monk'. These were the lay brothers, who did not take holy orders and who were drawn from the ranks of the labouring classes. Another fundamental belief of Bernard of Clairvaux was that the Cistercians should live a simple life in every appreciable way. This included a totally vegetarian diet and the building of extremely plain abbeys, with no towers or spires and absolutely no ornamentation whatsoever. In fact, in the early days of the Cistercian order, the monks did not even build their own abbeys. Labour was brought in from outside and was expected to work to the extremely austere plans laid down by Bernard of Clairvaux and his counterparts at Cîteaux in Burgundy.

Bernard of Tiron was no less pious than Bernard of Clairvaux and, if anything, his brothers lived an even harder life. There were no lay brothers in the Tironensian order, and everything was achieved by the choir monks themselves. Bernard of Tiron believed that although monks needed to live simple lives, they should be able to create and to craft beauty as a reflection of the gifts they had been given by God. This ability to *create*, especially in the form of building, should be offered back to God in terms of ornate and stunning abbeys, and also gifted to the communities in which they lived.

This meant that, right from the start, Tironensian abbeys were the last word in stunning architecture and ornamentation. In the beginning, Bernard of Tiron did all he could to encourage men who were already craftsmen to join his order. Most of his monks initially came from Brittany, though his first abbey was in France, not far from Chartres. Almost from the word go, Bernard of Tiron instigated training in the arts and crafts of building. Practical classes were held in the chapter-houses of the early Tironensian monasteries, and quite soon the order had created what amounted to a college of architecture and building in Chartres, where the order most probably took the lead in helping create the truly magnificent Chartres Cathedral, which was commenced in 1193. Chartres was an important religious centre, and it is said that since the 4th century, five successive cathedrals had been built on this site.

Whilst the Cistercians had it written into their very rules that they would not become involved in community activities or indeed even live alongside those who were not monks, the Tironensians were quite different. They were expert builders of bridges and churches, and they saw work in the community as being a way of passing on the religious message to those outside the monasteries, as well as being another form of prayer.

The efforts of Bernard of Tiron soon bore fruit because the Tironensians spread, initially at least, far faster than their Cistercian counterparts. Within only five years there were 117 Tironensian abbeys; most of these were in France, especially Brittany. Allowing for one example in the Welsh border, there were no Tironensian abbeys in England, but many in Scotland, Wales and Ireland. This state of affairs reflected the fact that Bernard of Tiron, and his order, preferred life in the Celtic fringes of the British Isles, mostly because of the order's Culdean leanings.

In 1113, the Tironensians established their first monastery in Scotland, at Selkirk. Legend has it that they were invited there by King Alexander I, brother of the more famous King David I. Quite soon they built another monastery in Kelso in 1128, Kilwinning in 1140 and Arbroath in 1178. The order was always popular with the Scottish Crown and many of the land grants they received originated with the kings of Scotland.

Culdean and Roman Christianity

At the time the Tironensians came to Scotland, and for some time afterwards, a quiet but insistent battle was taking place within the Church in Scotland. The origins of the problem dated back much earlier, to the 7th century. Prior to the 7th century all of the British Isles that was not pagan had practised a form of Christianity that was, in many ways, quite different from the form practised in Rome. It was Celtic in origin and though of course all Christians worshipped the Judaic Jesus,

Christianity in the British Isles had been partly left behind after the fall of the Roman Empire, as well as being to a great extent recreated by Irish and Scottish Christians during the Dark Ages. All over Ireland and Wales, and from the north of Scotland right down to the Midlands in England, the Celtic Church had predominated for several centuries. Most of the early Anglo Saxon converts to Christianity were Celtic Christians, converted by Scottish monks, and only the south of England had been peopled by missionaries from the Roman Church.

It is often stated that the main problem between the two Churches, Roman and Culdean, stemmed from the different way they chose to fix the date of Easter, but in reality there were a number of factors on which they did not agree. The sort of masses they celebrated, the way the churches were organized and the structure of monasticism all differed. This situation came to a head in 664 when a great Church gathering, known as the Synod of Whitby, took place in Yorkshire, in the north of England. At that time it was decided that England would recognize the Roman Church and its traditions. Annoyed and in disbelief, many of the Scottish monks simply went home and continued to worship as they had always done. The Moot Hill in Scone, where the Scots kings were crowned, was the place where the Pictish king dedicated a church to the Holy Trinity in AD 710. Following the Synod of Whitby the dedication of this Church was meant to be the official marriage of the Culdean and the Roman Church. From this union the mound received the name the Hill of Belief, but there is little doubt that Celtic Christianity continued to have a predominant part to play in Scottish Christian life for centuries beyond this date.

Roman Christianity actually caught up with Scotland when an Anglo Saxon princess named Margaret married the Scottish King Malcolm III around 1070. Margaret was a devout Roman Catholic and not a Culdean, but she was much loved in Scotland and eventually became St Margaret. Under her influence and that of her son, King David I, an attempt was made to gently persuade the Culdean Church, and especially its monks, to accept Roman ways. King David in particular seems to have believed that one way to do this was to introduce the Tironensians to Scotland. It was known that the Tironensians had strong leanings towards the Celtic Church, but they were, after all, Roman Catholic Benedictine monks.

If this was King David's plan, it seems to have backfired because, once ensconced in Scotland, the Tironensians appear to have become more Culdean than the Culdeans. This is not especially surprising. Their founder, Bernard of Tiron, was a rebel against Roman domination. Neither was he afraid to demonstrate the fact. Throughout his whole life he wore the hairstyle (tonsure) of a Celtic monk, which differed significantly from that of a normal Benedictine monk. Culdean monks shaved the front part of their head, but allowed the hair to grow at the back, whereas Roman Catholic monks shaved the middle of their head in deference to the crown of thorns worn by Jesus.

Bernard's insistence on the Celtic tonsure for both himself and his monks might seem like nothing more than a slight abstraction, but in reality it was a visible demonstration to the Church that this was a group of men who fully intended to go their own way and who would not toe the religious party line if they disagreed with it. There is evidence that the Celtic tonsure was worn in some Tironensian Scottish abbeys right up until the Reformation.

Fortunately, this silent religious rebellion, which was fought more in Scotland than anywhere else, never broke out into open warfare, but it is interesting to note that the Protestant Reformation came quite early to Scotland and that the Protestant faith was generally quite popular amongst ordinary Scottish people. Might this be a reflection of the fact that many Christian Scots were never *too* comfortable with Rome? Certainly there were periods when this seems to have been the case. In the days of the kingship of Robert the Bruce, not just he but the whole Scottish nation was effectively excommunicated for a protracted period. It was not until after the death of Bruce that the excommunication was rescinded. This came after the Battle of Teba, circa 1330 in southern Spain, in which most of the Scottish knights escorting the heart of Robert the Bruce on crusade, were killed in a valiant charge against the Moors. This brave charge changed the outcome of the battle in the favour of the Christians. Two Sinclair brothers were killed in this battle, which is reflected in a carved angel holding the heart and the death mask of King Robert the Bruce in Rosslyn Chapel.

The late King and Scotland were finally reconciled to the Church and the Pope but the nature and tenor of the Declaration of Arbroath (*see* Chapter Five) in 1320 amply demonstrates that the Scots would not tolerate treachery on the part of those who ruled them. There was a gentle but implied threat that this meant *any* ruler, possibly including a spiritual one such as a pope.

Of great interest is the fact that the person who is generally accepted as having written the Declaration of Arbroath was Bernard de Linton, a Tironensian and former Abbot of Kilwinning. Arbroath Abbey itself was also built and managed by the Tironensians. This Bernard was certainly a man of influence and did not allow the natural piety of a monk to get in the way of his political beliefs or allegiance. At the time he wrote the Declaration of Arbroath, he was Chancellor of Scotland! If he was anything like his namesake, Bernard of Tiron, he probably relished taking a sideswipe at the Pope.

With tremendous success, wealth and prestige, nearly all forms of reformed Benedictine monasticism eventually degenerated. This was certainly the case with the Cistercians, who gradually lost their primitive, abstemious life and became just as lax as other Benedictine orders before them. In fact, one of the reasons it was possible for King Henry VIII to seize the buildings and lands of all the English monasteries in the 16th century was because monks had become despised by many ordinary people who saw them as indolent, corrupt and parasitical.

Strangely, there is no indication that this was the case with the Tironensians; they were still working away in Scotland during the 1550s. By the time of the Scottish Reformation, the Tironensian abbeys still existed and the monks and their work were part of the Scottish landscape. Many a sturdy bridge, still standing, owes its existence to the Tironensians, likewise numerous parish churches. In most cases their involvement is not even recognized because they deliberately left no epitaph of their good deeds, partly because they believed to do so would denigrate their humility, but also because they considered that their attention to detail and the beauty of their finished stonework would be the best recognition of their skill, and their prayers to God. It did not matter to them if examples of their work were inaccessible and that no human eye could see their beautiful craftsmanship, for example along rooflines or in totally inaccessible corners. The craftsmanship was the same because God could see it and that is what mattered to them.

Gothic Architecture

The style of architecture typified by Rosslyn Chapel is known as Gothic. In a way, this term is unfortunate because it was originally coined as an insult by later architects who considered their own use of the classical style to be more advanced and to render the old style as being primitive. Since it was seen first in France, the true name of Gothic architecture should probably be 'Frankish architecture', but names stick.

What distinguishes Gothic architecture from the form that preceded it is one main factor – the shape of arches. The old style of church and civic building is known as Romanesque. Using rounded arches, Romanesque buildings had to be extremely strong and heavy. Romanesque churches can be recognized by their round arches, massive pillars and small window spaces. The advantage of the pointed arch in the Gothic style is that it displaces the load placed upon it in a different way to a round arch. In the case of large buildings, forces from above could be managed by using many pointed arches, and ultimately transferring much of the load outside the building to flying buttresses, which are more elegant than their predecessors and continue the theme of the pointed arch.

Handling loads better meant less masonry, which in turn led to less weight overall, allowing for greater window spaces because so much of the stress was being distributed by the arches and the flying buttresses. As a result, buildings soared upward, looked much more elegant and were seen as the height of modernity when compared with their solid, squat Romanesque counterparts.

The first recognized use of the Gothic arch was in Paris. It was in the church of Saint-Denis and is attributed to Abbot Suger, confidant of French kings and a powerful politician and churchman. Although Abbot Suger was brave enough to consider launching an entirely new style of architecture, nobody suggests that he was personally responsible for creating it. Neither are the Gothic features used at Saint-Denis in any way tentative or evolving. They can be seen in their full form and appear to have come from nowhere.

What might be significant is that Abbot Suger, as a young monk, had spent time at both Berneval-le-Grand in Normandy and in Toury, a little further inland. When travelling around the part of France where he had been sent, Suger could not have failed to come upon Tironensian monasteries, which already existed in this area. It is not impossible that he got to know the architect monks and called upon Tironensian experts when he eventually came to rebuild Saint-Denis, around 1135.

Certainly Gothic architecture was used extensively in the creation of Chartres Cathedral, which was commenced in part as early as the 1130s. It is virtually certain that the Tironensians had a hand in the creation of Chartres Cathedral, which, once the main part of the building was commenced in 1194, was completed in record time.

Nobody knows for sure where Gothic architecture actually came from. It is suggested that it might have developed as a result of Western travels to the East during the Crusades, because Islamic builders used a form of pointed arch. On the other hand, it may have simply been an innovation that came out of the head of some master craftsman in France. What we do know is that whilst the Cistercians continued to use Romanesque architecture in their own abbeys for some time after their founding, the Tironensians were soon proficient in the Gothic style. Bearing in mind the Tironensian obsession with building and also with learning, it is highly likely that Gothic architecture owes its existence to schools of building inspired and run by the Tironensian monks, either at Chartres or elsewhere. The fact that experts still do not know where the pointed arch developed would seem to be additional evidence that this was the case, since the Tironensians never laid personal claim to anything.

At the time Rosslyn Chapel was being planned, the Tironensian monks were still thriving in Scotland. Earl William Sinclair would have been very familiar with them, since at least one of their abbeys existed on his land. As we have seen in the case of Bernard de Linton and the Declaration of Arbroath, the Tironensians did not restrict themselves to their building projects – they were represented at Court, where Earl William would also have spent a large percentage of his time.

In fairness, having decided to create a new church on his land, Earl William could hardly have built it in any other style than the Gothic, which at the time was the norm. What sets Rosslyn Chapel apart from the average church being built in Scotland, or anywhere else during this period, is its complex nature – not simply in terms of its wonderful carvings but also with regard to its seemingly unnecessary complexity. The builders of Rosslyn Chapel did not content themselves with just one or two different forms of Gothic arch, but probably nearer 20; it is often said that Rosslyn contains every known style of arch to exist at the time it was built, which in so small a building is quite incredible.

It is not going too far to comment that someone was 'showing off' when the Chapel was created, since every stone-working technique available at the time seems to have been employed. Neither can the sheer quantity and quality of artistic carving be ignored. Rosslyn Chapel is a compendium of the stonemason's and stone carver's art as it existed in the middle of the 15th century, yet at the same time it is unique, and one of the facts that rebuts the involvement of foreign artisans is that there is nothing remotely like this structure anywhere on the European continent.

Having spent so long researching the Tironensian order – which sadly and unjustifiably has been all but bypassed by historians – there is no doubt in our minds that it was the Tironensian brothers, most likely from Kilwinning or Kelso, that Earl William used to create Rosslyn Chapel. Most likely, a local workforce provided the labour necessary, with the Tironensians being responsible for the overall design, the techniques used and probably the crispest and best of the carving. We freely admit that we have no definitive proof that this was the case, but on a balance of probabilities this seems to be the likeliest explanation.

Freestone and Freemasons

Such a theory would also seem to be substantiated by Rosslyn Chapel's long association with Freemasonry, a subject we will discuss at greater length presently. The very oldest of the world's Freemasons would seem to be those that originated in Kilwinning Abbey. Modern Freemasonry is almost certainly the speculative relation of a brotherhood of operative masons that first came into being in the chapterhouse of Kilwinning abbey as early as 1140. This has never been doubted in Kilwinning itself, which claims to have the oldest Freemasonic lodge in the world. When we consider that the word freemason, probably derived from 'freestone mason', Kilwinning's claim becomes even more set in stone.

Back in the days when almost every building of worth was created in stone, there were many different forms of artisans available to the builders of castles and churches. Much depended on the quality of stone available in any given area. If we take, for example, areas of East Anglia, in England, most architecture relied on the use of flint. When carefully arranged using mortar, flint can be used to build walls, but is neverthe-less utterly hopeless for carving. The same is true for certain types of sandstone, especially those possessing coarse grains. Different sorts of masons would have evolved in differing locations – people specialized in dealing with local materials and resultant local problems.

One such group were freestone masons who were probably the most skilled of all. These men dealt with fine-grained sandstone and, in particular, local stone that could be sawed successfully and used for both building and carving. Such stone is common in Scotland, and Rosslyn Chapel is built almost entirely of different shades of local sandstone.

The first known occurrence of a freestone mason being referred to as simply a 'freemason' is to be found in an Old French romantic story called 'Floris and Blancheflour', which was translated into Middle English between 1250 and 1300. This takes us back to a period not long after Kilwinning Abbey was built, and doubtless the word was in common use for some time prior to its appearance in print. The freemason mentioned in Floris and Blancheflour is not someone who turned up every Thursday night at his local lodge in order to participate in archaic and peculiar rituals – he was a working stonemason, but one conversant in the use of free stone.

This is exactly what the monks of Tiron were, as so many of their abbey ruins demonstrate admirably. What is more, since the word 'freemason' seems to have been in common use long before Rosslyn Chapel was built, it cannot be denied that those who created both its walls and its carvings were freemasons. How operative freemasons, of the sort that worked on Rosslyn Chapel, eventually became the speculative Freemasons of today is a story for later, but in a linguistic sense, at least, Rosslyn Chapel certainly owes its existence to free men who worked with freestone and were stonemasons.

✠ · ✠ · ✠

Slowly but surely we are beginning to see that Rosslyn Chapel is most definitely an expression of the time and place of its coming into existence. We have seen that although it is ostensibly a Christian foundation, it owes its presence to a particular *form* of Christianity, one that was peculiar to the Celtic fringes of Europe and especially to Scotland. At the same time, the men who envisaged and created it were not themselves Churchmen. Rather, they were well-read children of the Renaissance, whose interests extended into the realms of proto-science. The books at their disposal show that they were conversant with the classics, with mathematics, geometry, astronomy, alchemy and the Kabbalah. In this sense we can see that Rosslyn Chapel is as much a church of the mind as it is of any particular denomination – a university of collegiate chapels so to speak.

It is now time to go deeper into the symbolism of this remarkable building and to see what else it can tell us about Earl William Sinclair, Sir Gilbert Haye, the world in which they lived and the dreams that fuelled their actions. This library in stone still has much to tell us.

CHAPTER NINE

Into the Forest

There is no doubt in the minds of many of those who visit the place that Rosslyn Chapel lives and breathes as much in folklore and legend as it does in provable historical fact. This is perhaps inevitable and was undoubtedly part of the intention of those who created the structure. With their extensive library and the decidedly 'literary' bent of all the Sinclair lords, the family would have been fully conversant with a wealth of British traditions and stories, many of which ultimately date back to our most remote Celtic origins. Some of these were lifted from oral tradition into the written word, particularly the stories of the famed King Arthur, with which William Sinclair would have been quite familiar. It would not be surprising to discover that these glorious tales had a bearing on his thinking at the time Rosslyn Chapel was built.

Immediately to the north of the Scottish mainland are a group of islands known as Orkney. Although clearly part of Scotland, Orkney was under Scandinavian control for many centuries. As a result, the traditions of Orcadians owe as much to Norse culture and history as they do to that of the Celts.

Each year, on Christmas Day and New Year's Day, in

Kirkwall, capital of Orkney, locals take part in a game known as the ba'. The game involves two teams, known as the Uppies and the Doonies, comprised in the main of fit young men whose objective is to get a cork-filled leather ball either to a particular wall at the south end of the town or to the water of the harbour at the north end of Kirkwall. As with all such ancient community games, of which there are many examples in the British Isles, mayhem ensues, people are sometimes injured and doubtless much whisky is drunk.

Nobody has the faintest idea when the ba' began, though its ancient origins are not in doubt and it appears to have been a New Year game, which would have been celebrated on the day of the winter solstice, around 21 December. It is also generally accepted that the cork-filled leather ball used in the ba' game these days is a substitute for what was once an animal's head, or at times of conflict, gruesomely, the head of an enemy.

The ba' game is one example of what is generally referred to as the 'beheading game'. This, in turn, is almost certainly related to pre-Christian New Year celebrations. Perhaps fortunately, as it was once envisaged, the beheading game has now fallen into disuse, though remnants of its presence and the importance it once had to the people of the British Isles remains enshrined in some of our oldest and most poetic literature.

The Green Knight

The best example of a reference to the beheading game comes from a story entitled *Sir Gawain and the Green Knight*. This is part of the Arthurian tradition of literature, which was of the greatest importance in medieval times. King Arthur is a mythical or semi-mythical Celtic king, who was supposed to have fought against the Saxon invaders that eventually conquered England after the Roman withdrawal from the British Isles. Developing traditions had King Arthur keeping court at a place called Camelot, the real location of which, if there ever was one, is not known. In Camelot, King Arthur created a large round table and invited all the best knights of his kingdom and beyond to take seats at the table, as well as to joust, practise their skills at arms and to embark on adventures that often involved fair damsels or hideous dragon-like monsters.

Judging by the nature of the Middle English used in *Sir Gawain and the Green Knight*, it was probably written in the English Midlands and is thought to date to around the middle of the 14th century. In the story, Sir Gawain, one of King Arthur's knights, is present when the assembly in Camelot is approached by a mysterious warrior known as the Green Knight at the time of the New Year. The Green Knight, who, as his name implies, has a green face and wears green armour, insists that one of those present should strike him with a wonderful axe he is carrying, on the understanding that he will be able to return the blow on the next New Year's Day at a place called the Green Chapel.

The challenge is taken up by Sir Gawain, who does as he is bid. He decapitates his adversary and is then astounded when the Green Knight picks up his own severed head and leaves the assembly. A year later Sir Gawain sets forth, and, after a number of adventures of a typically Arthurian sort, he finds the Green Chapel and the Green Knight. Although Gawain bares his neck in order to receive the blow from the Green Knight, he suffers only a minor flesh wound. It is at this point, right at the end of the story, that the true theme of the beheading game is abandoned in favour of the more romantic and chivalrous ending appropriate to the literature of the period.

Like many of the Arthurian stories, the tale of *Sir Gawain and the Green Knight* was not entirely new or original when it was written in the 14th century. On the contrary, it owes its existence to much older stories concerning the beheading game. Many of these come from Welsh sources or from Ireland, and doubtless similar tales also existed in Scotland. They are, essentially, all parts of Celtic folklore and mythology, of which the beheading of an individual at New Year, followed by the beheading of another individual at the following New Year, is a typical example.

The decapitation of the head in these stories represents the severing of the old year. It is usually undertaken by a young man such as Gawain, who, in turn, must lose his own head at the end of the next year. The Gawain tale and similar stories are part of an even older belief that is to be found in the prehistory of many European cultures.

In Gawain's story, the Green Knight represents the old god, who was synonymous with the standing corn at harvest time. With the harvest, the corn is literally decapitated, and so the god of the corn dies. At the same time a new god (in this case Gawain) must take his place. Throughout the following year he gradually becomes the old god himself and he is eventually ritually killed as the corn at harvest time.

✥ · ✥ · ✥

The tale of Sir Gawain and the many similar stories that abounded were extremely popular in the 15th century when Rosslyn Chapel was created. Though often moral to some extent, these were secular stories that would have made entertaining reading after the literate person's usual diet of religious works of one sort or another. There are no such poems or stories amongst the Sinclair manuscripts that eventually found their way into the Bodleian Library, but Lord Fairfax certainly did not acquire the whole Sinclair library, some parts of which remain with the Scottish nation or in the hands of private collectors. Moving in courtly circles, at a time when chivalry was extremely popular and Arthurian tales were all the rage, Earl William cannot have been immune and, being an avid reader, probably did possess copies of these works.

Such themes may indeed have been in the minds of Earl William and Gilbert Haye as they sat down to plan the new Chapel, and, as we mentioned in our first book, *Rosslyn Revealed*, it isn't out of the question that Rosslyn Chapel, with its ample foliage, fruits and other nature aspects, was at least partly intended to represent the Green Chapel, where Gawain met the Green Knight.

The Green Man

One particular representation that regularly occurs in medieval carving definitely *does* seem to have a connection with these ancient themes of nature and seasons, and it is to be seen to a greater extent in Rosslyn Chapel than in any single structure anywhere in the world. This is the Green Man, who is usually represented as a face, from which emanates branches and foliage. Many ancient churches and civic buildings carry representations of the Green Man, carved either in wood or stone, but in Rosslyn Chapel there are literally dozens. It seems they are to be found in every nook and cranny of the Chapel, and it is unlikely that, even after so many years of searching, we have found them all.

The best and most exquisite of the Rosslyn Green Men are to be found amongst the stunning carvings in and around the retrochoir. Here they appear literally everywhere. In some cases they are carved openly onto stone bosses, whilst others are tucked into corners; in each and every case the face and foliage are different and unique. Some are smiling and benign, others are deliberately humorous, and still more are grotesque and obviously intended to disturb those who see them.

To understand why there are so many representations of the Green Man, both inside and outside the Chapel, we would first have to know *exactly* what the representation really means – or perhaps more correctly, what it *meant* to those who recreated it so many times. Many people think that the Green Man is a subconscious throwback to the pagan religion of our distant ancestors. We know, for example, that trees were of tremendous spiritual importance to our Celtic forefathers. Even as recently as the Iron Age, much of Britain was still heavily forested and Celtic religious ceremonies took place in forest groves. The English poet and historian Robert Graves showed in his book *The White Goddess* how the Celtic calendar had been based on trees and the Celts had many woodland deities.

Druids and Culdees

In the last chapter we made reference to the Culdees of Scotland – the peculiarly Celtic Christians, who had kept the faith alive during the long Dark Ages. Later, Culdee monks, who wore the Celtic tonsure, were not simply cocking a snook at the Roman Church. Rather, they were keeping alive a tradition that existed even before Christianity came to these shores. The priests of the Celts were called druids, which means 'oak seer', and they were the repositories of all of Celtic wisdom. Druids, who like the Culdee monks were priests, received a training of up to 20 years based at specific sites such as Angelsey in north Wales. After that they seem to have taken on a peripatetic life, travelling throughout the Celtic homelands. Amongst a clannish society in which intertribal fighting took place on a regular basis, druids stood outside of the tribal struggles and were considered sacred to all Celts. This gave them the right of safe passage, as well as the ability to arbitrate when trouble did break out.

The first Culdean monks served a broadly similar function. Many early Irish and Scottish monks were constantly on the move and probably enjoyed much the same status as the druids had done. Celtic Christianity held the same reverence for the natural world that seems to have been endemic in the pre-Christian Celts. The fact that there were similarities between the druids and their Christian counterparts, the Culdees, is not too surprising, being both a natural progression and also, doubtless, a strategy deliberately adopted by the monks themselves so that they might better suit the traditions of the people amongst whom they moved and also gain a degree of safety.

First and foremost, the Celts of the British Isles were farmers. Of course they were also famed warriors, but the basis of their existence depended on tilling the land for crops and upon keeping domestic animals. People at this time were not insulated from the natural world in the way we are now. Subsistence farming is hard, unremitting work, but it means those taking part in it are always close to the earth and are absolutely committed to the changing seasons.

It might be argued that very little actually altered when Christianity came to the Celtic heartland. No matter what deity was worshipped, corn had to be planted and cows had to be milked. In every respect the seasonal round remained the same, and this is amply reflected in the festivals of the Church. Christianity merely took universal ceremonies such as those at midwinter and midsummer, as well as the equinoxes, and placed its own relevance upon them. The Christian festival of Christmas, at which time Jesus is said to have been born, was merely the old festival of the winter solstice. Easter, the time of year at which it was said that Jesus died and was resurrected, comes at or around the time of the old spring equinox celebrations; harvest festivals replaced earlier times of feasting and reverence associated with the autumn equinox. Many important saints had their feast days set for other times in the year which had been important to pagans, such as St John the Baptist day on 24 June to coincide with the summer solstice, and his opposite saint, John the Evangelist, whose feast day used to occur at the midwinter solstice on 27 December, prior to the calendar changes instigated by Pope Gregory XIII.

The British humorist Israel Zangwill once said, 'Scratch a Christian and you will find a Pagan spoiled', and to a much greater extent than most Christians realize, this remains true, even today. The Green Man reflects this fact. He is certainly not peculiar to Scotland, but is to be found, in one form or another, all over the world. The fact that he occurs in such radically different cultures amply demonstrates just how old he must be. He was regularly to be seen on Roman inscriptions prior to the advent of Christianity, but became especially popular in Romanesque church architecture, and then later with the rise of the Gothic style. In a very few places such as the chapterhouse in Southwell Cathedral, Nottinghamshire, England, there are quite a few examples of Green Man images, but in the main he remains hidden away – often in corners of which only those who know a particular church well will be aware. Without doubt, Rosslyn Chapel holds the record for the most images of the Green Man to be seen in the same building, and whether or not we will ever fully understand what was in the mind of the stone carvers who rendered them, they were clearly of the utmost importance to the Chapel's planners. It has sometimes been suggested that gypsies, who have always been of importance to Rosslyn, may have been involved in the building and especially the carving. Their presence on the site, with their peculiar history and practices, might also go some way towards explaining the profusion of Green Man carvings.

Perhaps the best clue we have relates to the seasonal nature of the Chapel's adornment. John realized a long time ago that a *procession* of the seasons takes place around the Chapel's inner walls. For starters, you can see much more fruit and foliage in the east and south of the Chapel's interior. As the southern wall extends to its meeting with the western wall, this foliage and fruit becomes much less apparent, and it is even less obvious on the northern interior wall of the Chapel. At the same time, faces such as that of the Green Man, which appear in the east and south, show fecundity and growth. They are spring and summer, the youth in the east and the mature man in the south. Tendrils and branches emanating from their mouths and noses are fat and fleshy, and leaves are abundant. Autumn is the woody, bloated face full of ripe fruits and grain. Like the representation of fruit and flowers, a change takes place on the way round the inside of the Chapel until, on the north wall, the Green Man and other faces begin to take on a more grotesque look. Foliage is less apparent, faces become more drawn and older-looking until towards the north-facing parts of the Chapel there is a proliferation of skulls, implying corruption, death and winter.

To journey around the interior of the Chapel is to follow the seasons, from spring to summer, from summer to autumn and finally on to winter. When one bears in mind the precision with which the Chapel was placed on the landscape, and also the fact that it was specifically created to be responsive to the equinoxes, this isn't at all surprising. In the British Isles, and especially as far north as Scotland, it can readily be appreciated that the northern-facing walls of buildings are more weathered, pitted and inclined to be moss-covered than southern-facing walls. This is because it is from the north that the strongest and coldest winds come, and especially so in the winter months. In times gone by, when houses were open and draughty, with nothing approximating modern central heating, when food was in short supply and when the unremitting cold saw off the weakest members of society, the annual journey of the seasons to be seen inside the Chapel would have made eminent sense. No wonder, then, that the face of death is to be seen so regularly on the north or winter wall, whilst in the south, which is the direction from which the warm breezes of summer come, all is youthful, energetic and vibrant.

Undoubtedly, the most magnificent part of Rosslyn Chapel is the eastern end, the Lady Chapel or Holy of Holies as it is sometime called, not only on account of the sumptuous stone carvings it contains, but also because the biggest of the Chapel's windows shines down into that section of the building. Our ancestors undoubtedly saw the full scope of the passing year reflected in the cycles of day and night. To almost all cultures, even in the very remote past, the east, where the Sun, Moon and planets all rise on a daily basis, was always seen as the place of life and growth, whereas the west, where the heavenly bodies set, was the daily winter, with implications of foreboding and death. This was unmistakably taken into account in the original conception of the Chapel because, as we have seen, by far the most attention was lavished on the eastern section of the interior. The mediaeval day, with no mechanical clocks, extended from dawn to dusk, following the rising and the setting of the Sun, and this is reflected in a great many carvings in the chapel both internally and externally.

Overhead, the multitude of stars that adorn the whole of the interior of the barrel-vaulted roof, which itself mimics the great vault of the heavens, bear testimony to the intentions of the builders, who seem to have been virtually obsessed with the cycles of day and night, as well as those of the passing seasons. To recreate, in one's mind, what all of this must have looked like in its original form, when everything inside the Chapel was painted in rich colours, is to step back into the mindset of those whose original conception this was – an adoration for St Matthew was clearly present in their minds, whilst Judaic and Christian overtones are undeniably present, too.

CHAPTER TEN

Christianity's Cousin

I n our last book, *Rosslyn Revealed*, we drew attention to the striking similarities between the sort of Christians the planners and builders of Rosslyn Chapel seem to have been and some of the early denominations of Christianity, right back at the start of the faith. In particular, we looked closely at a very early group known as Ebionites, originating in and around Jerusalem. Ebionite Christianity remained rich in its Judaic origins, and they thought nothing of the later St Paul, whose travels and writing did so much to mould the eventual form of Christianity that was adopted across the Roman world and beyond. The Ebionites especially revered St Matthew; they had their own Gospel of St Matthew in Hebrew, and also doubtlessly available in Aramaic, which they claimed to be the original account of a genuine disciple of Jesus. Their version of St Matthew did not include the Nativity or other stories that the Ebionites considered were later additions to the Gospels.

Ebionites looked back to the founding of the first Temple by King Solomon – a theme that is echoed in Rosslyn Chapel

– and though the sect seems to have thrived in the early years after the life of Jesus, it eventually found itself at odds with the Latinized version of the faith that was developing outside of Palestine and especially in Rome. With so much that seemed to reflect Ebionite beliefs and thinking evident in Rosslyn Chapel with its St Matthew connection, we were forced to ask ourselves if some part of this original Christianity had survived, found its way to the west and become part of the extremely early Culdean Church that thrived in the Celtic homelands?

This had to be a possibility, but it did not answer all the questions thrown up by this most enigmatic of structures. There seemed to be something even more exotic at work – some sort of religious adherence that might be associated with Christianity, but which also had significant differences. In fact, there is one religion that would seem to explain Rosslyn Chapel admirably – not only the seasonal and cosmological accent of the building itself and its adornment, but it might also make sense of Rosslyn Chapel's undeniable importance to the creation and growth of Freemasonry.

Let's begin with a question: which religious figure was born of a virgin on 25 December, was accepted as the Son of God, had 12 followers, performed miracles, was killed and then resurrected, was known as 'the Light of the World', was celebrated with the eating of bread and the drinking of wine and had Sunday as his feast day?

OK, so you score well for saying Jesus, but you probably do not deserve maximum points because all the above was true of a mythological religious figure that predates Christianity. There are so many similarities between the Christian figure of Jesus and the earlier god Mithras that the developing Christian

Church had to take action in order to persuade its followers that Jesus was indeed the 'one and only' redeemer. It did so in a way that seems ridiculous to the modern mind. The early Church Fathers actually stated that the many similarities between Mithras and Jesus had come about because the Devil, always wishing to ensnare the unwary, had deliberately tampered with time, in order to make Mithras so similar to Jesus, though at an earlier date.

Logic asserts that the real reason for this state of affairs reflects an early Christianity trying to *assimilate* something that was a real threat to its own development. It had good reason to do so because Christianity and Mithraism vied to become the established and sole religion of a collapsing Roman world, badly in need of the glue that might be provided from a universally held belief system in a failing Empire.

So, who was Mithras, and if belief in his religion was so widespread that it nearly eclipsed Christianity, why do we know so little about it these days?

The story and figure of Mithras arose out of Zoroastrianism, once one of the world's most important faiths. The teachings of Zoroaster most probably date back to at least the 6th century BC and came from Persia (modern-day Iran).

Zoroastrianism is not entirely unlike other religions that developed from Abrahamic sources in that it accepts the concept of one God, and suggests that for the universe to move forward and progress it is necessary for individuals to live a good and virtuous life. The religion was practised over a wide area that fell under the control of the Roman Empire and so would have been quite familiar to most Roman citizens and openly practised by many.

The actual name Mithras dates back to at least the 6th century BC and is probably even older. It was originally attached to a Persian god, but did not take on the form in which the Romans knew it until shortly before the Christian era. At that time, a mystery religion began to develop, which was practised enthusiastically, not just in Rome itself but eventually across much, if not all, of the Empire. Because so little historical evidence remains, it has proved impossible to say with any certainty exactly where or when Mithraism first appeared. There are two reasons for this. Mithraism was a true *mystery* religion; its doctrines were probably never committed to the written word because by its very nature it depended on being passed on through word of mouth and example. In addition, the developing Christian Church was immensely hostile to Mithraism, and its authorities would have taken every opportunity to destroy any reference to Mithraic beliefs or practices.

Mysterious Mithraism

It is therefore almost impossible to discover anything concrete about Mithraism in terms of its true origins, or indeed its ultimate beliefs or practices. This is not unusual in the case of a mystery religion, which by its very nature was kept deliberately secret so that only initiates would receive its truths. A similar situation existed in the case of the Mysteries of Demeter, which were practised for many centuries at Eleusis in Greece and which had tens of thousands of devotees at any one time. The Demeter Mysteries were enacted each year, at the time of the autumn equinox. Devotees had to undergo a series of ritualized experiences that may or may not have been made all the more real by the ingestion of hallucinogenic drugs, most probably from ergot fungi. At the end of their 'ordeal' initiates were introduced to the *true* mysteries of the Demeter cult. At the same time they were warned that passing on to the uninitiated any part of the ceremony they had undergone would lead to execution. Since we know even less about the Mysteries of Demeter than we do about the Mysteries of Mithras, we can take it that people took the threat very seriously and, indeed, it is known that people were sometimes killed for talking about the Demeter Mysteries to those who had not experienced them.

Most of what remains regarding Mithraism is representational and is to be seen on carvings, steles, etc, that have been found in various places throughout the Roman Empire. It has often been suggested that Mithraism was especially favoured by Roman soldiers, and though this may be true, it could also *seem* to be this way because evidence of Mithraic practice has turned up in archaeological sites in places where Roman soldiers were garrisoned. In other words, Roman soldiers may have spread Mithraism, but were probably not its only adherents.

It is possible to make a stab at some of the beliefs of Mithraism from the pictographic evidence that remains, especially where the same themes occur in many different places. It appears that Mithras was a god that took a particular interest in the affairs of humanity. He may have been, in many respects, a character similar to Jesus in that he is often referred to as 'the Son of the Living Sun', whereas Jesus is referred to as 'the Son of the Living God'. There doesn't seem to be any doubt that both Greek and Persian mythology played a part in the rise of

Mithraism because Mithras is often depicted in close associa-tion with the Greek Sun god Helios.

As far as the birth of Mithras is concerned, there are some variations. He was said to have been born of a virgin and appeared either out of a rock, or a tree, around which was coiled a serpent. Mithras is often naked in such scenes, but is almost always wearing a Phrygian cap – a conical hat that falls over at the point. This type of hat is also closely associated with the Roman goddess Libertas, and the Phrygian cap became synonymous in history with the freeing of slaves and, later, the search for liberty and freedom from oppression. Because Mithras wears such a cap, we can take it that being initiated into the Mysteries of Mithras inferred a freedom from 'something' – most likely, in tune with the Mysteries of Demeter, a freedom from death that comes with a true understanding of creation and the godhead.

The most common scene relating to Mithras is one in which he is shown slaying a bull. It is possible that the bull represents demonic forces or the Mithraic representation of evil. There are also representations of Mithras making a meal of the bull with Helios, the Sun god, who we can take as representing his father. Mithras performed miracles whilst he was living amongst humanity. In particular, he is often shown firing an arrow at a rock, from which fresh water emerges. At the end of his time amongst humanity, Mithras was taken up into heaven in a chariot.

In truth, this is not a lot to go on. We do also know that because he was essentially a solar deity, the day of the week held as being sacred to Mithras was Sunday, and, for similar reasons, he is said to have been born on 25 December, which in the Roman world had long been a date associated with the birth of the Sun – obviously because it represented the winter solstice, at which time the Sun ends its journey south along the eastern horizon and once more begins to move north, towards summer. In addition, historians are aware that bread and wine were significant symbols in Mithraism and that these, as well as other foods, were consumed in meals related to the Mystery celebrations.

Mithras and the Zodiac

One series of possible facts regarding Mithras is particularly important in terms of our present research, and it stems from the theories of David Ulansey, Professor Emeritus of Philosophy and Religion at the California Institute of Integral Studies, in San Francisco. A great deal of the pictographic evidence tends to associate Mithras with the zodiac, which of course probably isn't too surprising if his father was the Sun. Professor Ulansey noted the cosmological aspects of Mithraism and balanced these against the fact that Mithraism, though based on old names and old religious traditions, seems to have been a new departure, deliberately created in Rome and dating back to the first part of the 1st century AD.

Ulansey came to the conclusion that the evolution of the Mysteries of Mithras related specifically to the discovery by the Greek astronomer Hipparchus (c. 190 BC–c. 120 BC) of a natural occurrence known as the precession of the equinoxes. Prior to the time of Hipparchus it seems to have been generally held that the positions of the stars, as seen from the Earth, never altered. Hipparchus knew from his own observations that this wasn't true and he was able to calculate how an Earth-bound view of the skies would alter across time. This is due to the fact that the Earth wobbles on its axis over a very long period, somewhat like a child's spinning top. The result is that our view of the stars changes across the centuries and Hipparchus was able to calculate that the point of the equinoxes was moving backwards through the zodiac at around 1° per century. He wasn't far out because we now know that the full precession of the equinoxes takes around 26,000 years.

Ulansey believes that as knowledge of the discoveries of Hipparchus spread throughout the Roman Empire, the revelation regarding the precession of the equinoxes took on a religious proportion. He suggests that it inferred in the minds of some people that a new deity had been discovered which was causing the precession. After all, a deity capable of moving the heavens in their entirety would be worth following; this role was filled by Mithras.

Evidence of this theory is cited as being played out in the bull-slaying scenes associated with Mithraisim (known as tauroctonies), which are remarkably similar, no matter where they have been found. They always contain specific details such as Mithras himself, a dog, a snake, a scorpion and a raven. What is more, there is nearly always direct astronomical iconography associated with pictures or sculptures relating to Mithraism. On many occasions the whole zodiac is shown, as are the Sun and Moon. Taken altogether this may prove to be important because if we take the bull in the bull-slaying scene to be representative of the zodiac sign of Taurus, then all the other creatures present make sense in terms of other constellations of stars that exist across a continuous band of the sky, including Taurus itself. The dog would be Canis Minor, the snake would be Hydra, the raven would be Corvus, and the scorpion would be Scorpio. Mithras is also invariably shown with two male attendants and these could represent the zodiac sign of Gemini.

This all begins to make more sense in light of the considerations of a Neo-Platonic philosopher by the name of Porphyry (c. AD 234–c. AD 305). He wrote about a cave that lies at the heart of the stories of Mithras. This was the place where Mithras killed the bull and shared it with the Sun god. Porphyry suggested that ancient sources, now lost to us, had declared the cave was intended to be an image of the cosmos. This is substantiated by Zoroastrianism, which portrays Zoroaster finding such a cave himself and also treating it as a microcosm of the universe.

All of this fits very neatly with mithraea that have been located in various parts of the Roman Empire. Mithraea were the rooms in which devotees of Mithras met, in order to carry out their rituals. All were meant to represent artificial caves and had barrel-vaulted roofs. Mithraea are not large, typically holding 30 to 40 participants, and most, if not all, were created specifically to serve the Mithraic function. If such artificial caves were created to represent the heavens, it is appropriate that they possessed barrel-vaulted roofs, which themselves could be taken as the vault of heaven above the head of any individual looking up on a dark night. This fact also bears out the theories of Professor David Ulansey.

Precession of the Equinoxes

As Ulansey points out, in the Graeco-Roman world, the view of the cosmos as espoused by the learned men of the time was of a geocentric universe. In other words, they firmly believed that the Earth was fixed and that all of space revolved around it as a great sphere. Every day the sphere of heaven, with the stars attached to it, circled around the static Earth, taking with it the Sun, Moon and planets, all of which also had independent movement. It was believed that the Sun travelled around the Earth once each day with the sphere, but it also had its own movement, which caused it to describe a path through the background stars that remained broadly the same, from one year to the next. In the minds of the observers and for the sake of tracking the heavenly bodies, the path the Sun took throughout the year was split into 12 sections, all of which contained groups of stars known as constellations. The 12 major constellations that split the great circle that was the path of the Sun were known as the zodiac. Each one attracted a name and a mythology, roughly based on its shape and the creature or individual it was thought to portray.

Ancient astronomers knew very well in what part of the zodiac the Sun should appear at any given time of year, so when Hipparchus demonstrated that this was changing very slightly, across a long period of time, it seemed to the observers that *something* had the power to move the whole universe.

Because the Earth does not sit straight up, relative to its orbit of the Sun, but rather has an angle of around 23.4°, the circle formed by the zodiac, and therefore the Sun's yearly path, and the circle that represents the celestial equator, do not match. However, twice each year they cross, and for a day the Sun stands on the celestial equator. These are the spring and autumn equinoxes, and they were of tremendous importance to ancient astronomers in tracking and rectifying the Sun's movements, and therefore the calendar.

The presence of the precession of the equinoxes effectively means that the points in the zodiac at which equinoxes appear, change very slightly over a long period of time. When Hipparchus was conducting his research, the spring equinox was in the zodiac sign of Aries, whereas now it is in Pisces and moving backwards, year by year, towards Aquarius.

What is interesting about all this is that the zodiac signs and other constellations represented in the Mithraic tauroctonies represent the state of play as far as the equinoxes were concerned between about 4000 BC and 2000 BC, during which time the spring equinox appeared in the sign of Taurus, the bull, whereas the autumn equinox was in Scorpio, the scorpion. Just as interesting is the fact that in some versions of tauroctonies, two other symbols other than the ones mentioned above are included. These are the representation of a lion and a cup. These additions add weight to Ulansey's theories because they could so easily represent Leo, the lion, where the summer solstice would have occurred between 4000 BC and 2000 BC, and Aquarius, the water carrier, which marked the winter solstice during the same period.

It stands to reason that at the time Mithraism came into existence, if certain people *knew* that the spring equinox was no longer happening in Taurus but rather in the previous zodiac sign of Aries, then the bull was effectively dead – in other words, it was 'sacrificed' in favour of the ram of Aries. And since only an extremely powerful god could move the entire universe, it was this god that was effectively slaying the bull. Having recognized this, it would be sensible for those who understood this new astronomical mystery, to worship the god in question – which is how Mithras came about.

Believers in Mithras undoubtedly accepted that any god capable of moving the entire universe must originate and dwell outside of that universe. In a way, this makes Mithras not so different from Jesus, who we are told was a manifestation of God. The God of Judaism and Christianity is just such a figure who, unlike the pagan gods of old, does not live on a mountain top or in the depth of the ocean but rather in a realm outside of our universe. This might all seem self-evident to us now, but it was a positive revolution in thinking to the minds of the time.

A Mystery Religion

So why did Mithraism become a mystery religion? Why was it not practised openly, attracting dogmas and a theology as other faiths had done throughout history? There could be a few reasons for this. Firstly, Mithraism came about at a time when mystery religions were the fashion. Many people followed the Mysteries of Demeter and the Egyptian Mysteries of Isis – but there were also others. (Christianity itself contains all the requisite components to be termed a mystery religion, a fact that is hardly denied by its adherents who talk regularly about the 'mysteries' of the faith.) Mystery religions differed from the large, state-sponsored beliefs that revolved around old gods such as Jupiter or Mars. Because they offered 'the secrets or mysteries' that could only be passed on by someone who was already initiated, they had a degree of exclusivity that the bigger, more traditional religions did not.

It was also possible in most cases for participants in mystery religions to rise quickly to a rank from which they could 'dispense' the mysteries to others, so the priesthood was not generally exclusive. At the same time, most of the mystery religions dealt in the thorny problem of life and death, offering individual salvation and a direct communion with the godhead.

Finally, the mystery religions were more closely related to tribal ceremonies and rites of passage than the larger, more authoritarian religions were. This offered a sense of 'inclusivity' and, in the case of Mithraism, might go part of the way to explaining why Mithras was always displayed wearing the Phrygian cap – the cap of freedom. This symbol was also later used as a symbol of the French Revolution.

As far as can be ascertained, only men could take part in the Mysteries of Mithras. Some experts suggest that women could be included in certain places, and under specific circumstances, but there is little evidence that this was ever the case. As to the actual doctrines, the words spoken during initiations, or the ultimate promise of Mithraism, we can have no idea. What we *do* know is that Mithraists slowly worked their way through seven degrees of initiation. Each of these doubtless had its own trials and ceremonies, and though we are not aware what these might have been, except that both physical and mental feats were expected of initiates, we do know what they were called.

1. The Raven or Crow. Its symbols were a beaker or a cup and it was associated with the planet Mercury.

2. The Male Bride, the symbols of which were a lamp, a bell, a veil and a crown. This was responsive to the planet Venus.

3. The Soldier, the symbols of which were a pouch, a helmet, a lance, a drum, a belt and the chest plate. It was responsive to the planet Mars.

4. The Lion. The symbols were a musical instrument called a sistrum, a laurel wreath and thunderbolts. The planetary significance in this case was to Jupiter.

5. The Persian. The symbols were the Phrygian cap, a sickle, moons and stars, and a sling pouch. The planetary ruler was the Moon.

6. The Sun-runner. Its symbols were a torch, images of Helios, the Sun god, whips and robes. In terms of heavenly bodies it was associated with the Sun.

7. Pater (the Father). The symbols in this case were a mitre, a shepherd's staff, a garnet or ruby ring, and elaborate robes carrying gold and silver threads. In terms of planetary symbolism it was responsive to Saturn.

It would be wonderful to be party to the ceremonies that ran alongside all of these degrees of initiation, or to know what aspirants talked about or the feats they undertook during their meetings, but it is unlikely that this will ever be the case. The developing Christian Church, first of all, went to great trouble to bring aspects of Mithraism into its own beliefs, dogmas and practices, and then, when it became more powerful, it endeavoured to destroy Mithraism wherever it still existed.

Christianity probably won out over Mithraism in part because it was more inclusive. Anyone could be a Christian, whether they were male or female. Social class was irrelevant, as was profession or background. At the same time, it has to be considered that there is so much of Mithraism in Christianity that it eventually offered a safe haven, even to those people who were Mithraists. Christianity is not based on cosmological precepts and is therefore less intellectually based than Mithraism seems to have been, but in one way or another it appears to be incredibly similar. We will probably never be certain just how much early Christianity was changed in order to accommodate its immediate rival, but if the reader looks again at the list at the beginning of this chapter, it becomes obvious that it bent over backwards to offer believers in Mithras a viable alternative.

Mithraism and the Chapel

So what, if anything, could the mystery religion of Mithras have to do with Rosslyn Chapel? There is a persistent and oft-quoted rumour concerning Rosslyn Chapel that it stands on the site of an earlier structure. It has been suggested that this was a mithraeum (though it has proved impossible to trace the source of this suggestion).

How likely is this? Firstly, it has to be remembered that the Romans who conquered Britain did not hold, for any length of time, the part of Scotland where Rosslyn Chapel stands. Although they made punitive expeditions into Scotland, and even created a wall further north than Midlothian in the early days of their occupation, they eventually settled on retreating to the biggest and final wall between the River Tyne in the east and the Solway Firth in the west – well below Midlothian. Whilst this does not make a mithraeum at the site of Rosslyn Chapel an impossibility, it might be seen as unlikely. However, following the River Esk which flows through Rosslyn Glen just below the Chapel to the point it meets the sea at Musselburgh, there was an important Roman settlement at Inveresk, so maybe the Romans were in the area long enough to establish a mithraeum. But why should anyone have made this suggestion in the first place?

Rosslyn Chapel has always been closely associated with Freemasonry, and the idea that it may be connected in some way with Mithraism is likely to have come from the direction of a Freemasonic researcher. This is because there are great similarities between Freemasonry and Mithraism. Researchers in the Victorian period particularly were at pains to point out that, for example: Mithraism had degrees of initiation, as does Freemasonry; Mithraism was exclusive to men, as indeed was Freemasonry until very recently. Freemasonry has initiation promises and oaths that are broadly similar to those known to have existed amongst the mystery religions, which were undoubtedly present in Mithraism. Freemasonry claims to be extremely ancient, as is Mithraism, and although the name of Mithras is never specifically mentioned in Freemasonic ritual, this is hardly surprising. With the Christian Church so antagonistic towards Mithras, any mention of the name could have spelled disaster for individual Freemasons and for their Craft as a whole.

If Freemasonry is genuinely as old as it purports to be, it could easily represent a corrupted version of Mithraism – one that was altered enough to avoid falling foul of accusations of heresy. Of course, in the present era, the Catholic Church has no power to interrogate or execute anyone, so if Freemasonry is Mithraism in a cloak, why does it not come clean about what it truly represents? The obvious answer to this question is that nobody within Freemasonry remembers what it once was.

Let us suppose, just for the sake of the exercise, that Mithraism did survive in a secret form – which would not have been too difficult bearing in mind that it 'dealt' in secrets and mysteries – and that many of its core beliefs had been usurped by the Christian Church. As long as its existence was not revealed to the religious authorities, it would probably have had little difficulty in continuing, generation after generation. Neither is it beyond credibility that in the fullness of time it would ally itself to a craft guild, such as that of freemasons – the stonemasons who specialized in working freestone.

Guilds were, to a great extent, secret societies in any case. Individual skills such as those possessed by masons, cutlers, silversmiths, goldsmiths, etc, were regularly referred to in medieval times and after as 'mysteries'. Guilds were trade associations, but were extremely tight-knit organizations. They expected the children of their members to intermarry wherever possible, and this invariably happened. As we saw in Chapter Two, proponents of individual trades often occupied the same streets in towns and cities, had their own churches and socialized within their own tight circles. All of this ensured that the secrets of a profession remained within the possession of guild members and did not pass to outsiders who were not party to the trade's 'mysteries'.

Aspects of Mithraism could easily have survived within a tight-knit guild, although because certain specific details such as the name of Mithras and the exact circumstances surrounding his worship could not be divulged, for fear of spies being present, they could instead be *hidden* inside another story such as that of the building of the Temple of Solomon. As the Church grew more powerful and as heresy became the stuff of Catholic witch hunts, the inner secrets of this 'brotherhood' would have to be more and more safeguarded. The result, after many generations, would undoubtedly be that the original truth of the fraternity would be lost, leaving only the stories it had used to disguise its real and original intentions.

This is exactly what Freemasonry seems to be – in modern parlance it might be called 'a rebel without a cause'. Its moral imperatives remain, as do a whole series of mythical stories relating to Solomon's Temple and its creation, but the very heart of the fraternity appears to be missing. All Freemasons have to swear that they believe in 'something', but the true nature of the something in question is not specified – or is it?

Rosslyn specialized in promoting the guilds at the time of William Sinclair and Sir Gilbert Haye; in fact, they produced and reproduced more than a few books which leaned in this direction, such as the *Buik of the Law of Arm's*, *The Buke of tile* and *The Buke of the Governaunce of Princes*, from a French version of the pseudo-Aristotelian *Secreta secretorum*, a guide to how a king should treat his subjects. Chivalry, fraternity and humanitarianism lay at the heart of the collected works of Sir Gilbert Haye. Rosslyn became an important centre of mediaeval trade guilds; artisans from all over Europe were working there, even goldsmiths were listed as being present in the late 1450s; they are recorded in commissions making gold chalices for both Rosslyn Chapel and St Magnus Cathedral in Orkney. It became a centre for the creation of the arts and was fertile ground for the development of the trade guild organizations and their attendant secrets.

CHAPTER ELEVEN

In the Crypt

If we are ever going to understand why the relationship between Rosslyn Chapel and Freemasonry came about, we need to learn more about what truly inspires Freemasonry and what actually lies at its heart. This might, in the end, offer us the best clues of all regarding the motivations of those who put this strangest of churches on the Scottish landscape, and it could even tell us why they were so keen to dedicate their Chapel to St Matthew.

Freemasonry describes itself not as a secret society but rather as a society with secrets. In reality, there is little information regarding Freemasonry that cannot be discovered by anyone who chooses to surf the Internet and spend a few hours looking at the relevant sites, though what the average person discovers will probably not mean much to them. Freemasonry is so wreathed in allegory and suffused with apparently ancient symbolism that even very few Freemasons understand a great deal of what goes on around them at the average lodge meeting.

Freemasonry began, according to the Grand Lodge of England, in the 18th century, but this is only part of the story because it relates to the time when a group of already existent

Freemasonic lodges came together in London to create Grand Lodge. This, of course, means that Freemasonry *did* exist before the nominal date of 1717. As we have seen, in the estimation of at least some Scottish Freemasons, the first lodge was created in the 12th century, at Kilwinning, though we have no way of knowing whether this was any more than a very early association of stonemasons – a sort of proto-guild.

According to its central themes and traditions, Freemasonry is much older than even the Kilwinning lodge because it is supposed to have started with the masons who built Solomon's Temple in Jerusalem, and this would put the date back to around 1000 BC. However, not even many Freemasons consider that the stories of the Craft relating to Solomon and his Temple are anything other than fables, and it appears to be the case to most rational people that these central themes of Freemasonry are what they appear to be – various forms of allegory, used to explain the moral precepts upon which Freemasonry is actually based.

As far as the practice of Freemasonry is concerned, in order to be a full member of a lodge, a man (or a woman these days) must pass through three degrees, each with its own rituals and symbols, before becoming a full-fledged Freemason. These degrees are known as 'Entered Apprentice', 'Fellow Craft' and 'Master Mason'. Each degree has its own rituals and symbols. The structure of the language used in these ceremonies tends to be quite archaic, and over the centuries nobody seems to have made any strenuous effort to bring it up to date or to remove sections that are no longer relevant. This is partly because tradition plays such an important part in Freemasonry, but it also means that the real *truth* behind certain rituals and speeches is never lost inadvertently. But as an example of the redundant parts of Freemasonry we have the horrible oaths associated with the Craft, detailing the punishment that will be handed out to any Freemason, who betrays the Craft's secrets. These may have meant something once upon a time, but like so much else in the Craft they now merely form part of a romantic backdrop to the ceremonies of the lodge.

The rank of Master Mason is as far as anyone can go in Freemasonry, but there are other associated bodies that offer additional degrees. These are ancillary to the three essential degrees, and in most cases anyone seeking them must be a Master Mason before proceeding. In Scottish Rite Freemasonry, of the sort practised extensively in the United States, it is possible to achieve 33 different degrees; these days, degrees are often awarded in blocks of two or more to cut down on the time involved and the amount of ceremony that has to be learned.

✠ · ✠ · ✠

Neither John nor Alan are Freemasons, though this has not precluded an interest in the Craft and extensive research both individually and together. Alan has published a number of books related to Freemasonry, and readers who want to go into the subject in greater detail might look at *The Goddess, the Grail and the Lodge*[1] or *The Hiram Key Revisited.*[2]

Like most people researching the subject we wanted to know what, if anything, lay at the heart of Freemasonry. Freemasonic agencies are unanimous in declaring that the Craft, as it is called, is definitely not a religion. Each prospective Freemason must profess a belief in a deity of some sort, though no specifics are mentioned, and in Freemasonry the deity is referred to as 'The Great Architect of the Universe' or 'The Grand Architect of the Universe'. So we can assume that a specific religious imperative was either *never* involved in Freemasonry, or else it has been deliberately obscured, possibly for so long that even members of the Craft are now unaware of it.

Freemasonry and Astronomy

Most of those who looked hard at Freemasonic symbols and analysed the rhetoric have arrived at the conclusion that what plays the biggest part in the 'undertones' of Freemasonry is astronomy. This is apparent at many different levels, and much of the evidence for an astronomical structure was rooted out back in the 19th century by an American Freemason called Robert Hewitt Brown. The result of his exhaustive research was a book entitled *Stellar Theology and Masonic Astronomy*[3] which, although originally published in 1882, was recently republished and so is available to modern researchers. Well over a hundred years on it still makes fascinating reading.

Hewitt Brown came to the conclusion that Freemasonry was based almost exclusively on astronomy, and Sun worship in particular. Most modern researchers who go deep enough into Freemasonry tend to agree with him. Everything about the Craft shouts astronomy. For example, every lodge must be situated on an east–west axis. When asked why this is so, Dr Hemming, an eminent Victorian American Freemasonic researcher said: 'Because the Sun, the glory of the Lord, rises in the east and sets in the west.'

A lodge also has three lights, one in the east, another in

the south and a third in the west. This is to match the journey of the Sun during any given day because it rises in the east, gains its highest point in the south and then sets in the west. Freemasons are also instructed to travel to the east, because that is where the Sun rises.

One of the most important symbols in Freemasonry is known as the Royal Arch. Whilst on the one hand the arch is an architectural feature, the Royal Arch in Freemasonry represents the arch of heaven. It runs from the spring equinox to the autumn equinox, passing through the summer solstice.

Time and again in Freemasonry, and at every level, cosmology turns out to be the most important underlying factor in both symbolism and ceremony. Hewitt Brown even goes so far as to suggest that Freemasonry's most famous mythical character, Hiram Abif, represents the Sun.

This almost total reliance on astronomy isn't always evident to those who take the degrees. Astrological truths in Freemasonry are almost always obscured by allegory, and it sometimes takes a practised eye and a good understanding of historical astronomy and astrology to understand what is really going on.

Symbolism and Ritual

In our own era, when to talk about almost anything publicly is allowed, and when we are not constrained by powerful religious forces that once dictated everything we were permitted to say, the cosmological nature of Freemasonry has become known to all researchers. A few centuries ago this would not have been the case. The similarities between Freemasonry and Mithraism are so obvious that practitioners would have been in danger of being hauled before the Inquisition. Therefore those involved thought up a different strategy, which allowed them to follow their own beliefs – but in a disguised way. A fraternity based on cosmology might have attracted attention and strenuous further investigation, but one concerning itself primarily with architecture and geometry would not.

At the heart of Freemasonry, apparently at least, is the Old Testament of the Bible and especially its stories about King Solomon. What could possibly be suspect about any organization based upon biblical stories? In reality, the Church has always suspected and mistrusted Freemasonry, and probably with good cause, especially when one realizes that the name Solomon, though purporting to mean 'peaceful and perfect', actually translates as 'man of the Sun'.

The way Freemasonry was organized meant that those first entering the Craft had little idea what all the ritual and symbolism really meant. This remains the case today, and it is the fraternal and social aspects of Freemasonry that have always attracted most members. Having achieved even the third degree, the average Freemason could, and still can, remain absolutely ignorant regarding the true nature of the 'club' he has joined; only those people who embarked on a diligent search would achieve a genuine understanding of what lies at the heart of Freemasonry. Since to really understand Freemasonry requires a good understanding of astronomy, which can be a difficult subject to master, most people didn't, and don't, bother.

The truth is that there are so many similarities between Freemasonry and what we know of Mithraic beliefs, the only essential difference is that Freemasonry has hidden its true purpose and philosophy, which it had to do in order to survive in difficult times.

✛ · ✛ · ✛

The question we asked at the start of this chapter was why has there always been a tangible link between Freemasonry and Rosslyn Chapel? In reality, we have not been able to discover a specific church anywhere in the world that has been so closely linked to Freemasonry. We know that this association is not modern. It has nothing to do with the mystery surrounding the Chapel that has been so apparent in recent years and which was amplified by the book and film *The Da Vinci Code* because the connection extends back in time as far as we are able to see.

The Sinclair family, builders of Rosslyn Chapel, have had a long and illustrious association with Freemasonry. As early as 1736, Sir William Sinclair of Rosslyn resigned as the hereditary Grand Master of Freemasonry in Scotland, because the Craft had organized itself and created the Grand Lodge of Scotland. It appears that he did not wish to force himself upon what was becoming a democratic and formalized body. The fact that he did so suggests that the family's association with Freemasonry was already old at that time. The Sir William in question said:

> … that the Masons in Scotland did, by several deeds, constitute and appoint William and Sir William St. Clair of Rossline, my ancestors and their heirs, to be their patrons, protectors, judges, or masters …

This statement would seem to suggest that *all* the Sinclairs of Rosslyn had been hereditary masters of Scottish Freemasonry, which itself adds weight to the speculation that the Craft *began* at Rosslyn and that the St Clairs (later the Sinclairs) had been the protectors and perhaps even the creators of the Craft.

If this is the case and if Freemasonry is, in reality, a disguised version of Mithraism, is there anything at Rosslyn Chapel that would prove the connection? Indeed there is and it takes us back to the very dedication of Rosslyn Chapel, to St Matthew.

We need first to look again at the story regarding St Matthew that led to most of the sumptuous and even breathtaking stone carving to be seen at the Chapel's east end. This is the story of St Matthew visiting the city of Myrna, where he performed a miracle that resulted in a fountain being created and to a great tree growing, which offered food and shade to the citizens of Myrna.

The reader will recall that this story is not to be found in the Bible. It is contained in a great body of work known as the *Ante-Nicene Fathers*, a collection of stories that developed and appeared at various times after Christianity became a religion. The Bible itself tells us very little about St Matthew, nor indeed many of the central characters in the New Testament. It is probably therefore not surprising that further stories regarding St Matthew and others evolved to feed the appetites of believers. Whether many of the stories in the *Ante-Nicene Fathers* are true seems to be irrelevant. They have been adopted by the Church and, in historical times at least, were *treated* as though they were reliable accounts of actual happenings.

At face value there is nothing especially odd or different about the tale of St Matthew at Myrna; accounts of miracles being performed by the Evangelists and disciples in the years after the death and resurrection of Jesus are common. But in light of what we know about Mithraism, this particular story is worth another look because there are striking parallels between St Matthew's actions at Myrna and information we have regarding Mithras and some of his deeds and exploits.

We are told that upon arriving in the city of Myrna, St Matthew stood upon 'a certain lofty and immovable stone'. After giving a lengthy speech Matthew planted his staff into the ground (which logically must have been the stone). Immediately the staff grew into a massive tree, with vines spiralling around it. The story describes the tree in detail and also tells us that 'a fountain of water came forth from the root of it'.

Now let us look at what we know of Mithras – which admittedly isn't a great deal, but there are some facts that appear so frequently on statues and carved inscriptions that we can be certain they were part of the Mithraic traditions. One of these is a regularly portrayed miracle that Mithras performed. In order to bring the world to life, Mithras fired an arrow at a rock, and from the rock emerged a fountain of water.

We also know from carvings and inscriptions that Mithras himself was thought to have been born from a rock. He is invariably shown in human form, but sometimes as a tree or pillar, and there is nearly always a snake entwined around the emerging Mithras.

The parallels are striking, and it begins to look as though the story of St Matthew at Myrna is a garbled retelling of parts of earlier stories that were not Christian at all but rather Mithraic. This would not be too surprising because the early

Church regularly hijacked religious sites, pre-Christian deities and mythological tales, and regurgitated them to suit its own needs.

We also know from the story that St Matthew was ultimately martyred in Myrna, though it is clear that he willingly gave himself up to this fate because earlier in the story he defied all attempts to put him to death. Like all good saints and martyrs, including Jesus, St Matthew died so that others might benefit. He was, in effect, a conscious sacrificial victim. The same was also true of Mithras. According to Charles-François Dupuis (1742–1809) a French savant, professor, mathematician and expert in mythology, particularly in Persian mythology, Mithras was crucified on 22 March and rose again three days later on 25 March. Dupuis cites annual re-enactments of this happening being played out in Persia. Followers believed that Mithras was the saviour of humanity – in much the same way Christians believe that Jesus is the saviour of mankind.

It is true that the story of St Matthew at Myrna has been thoroughly Christianized, in that it also includes Jesus as part of the cast, but we believed from the first time we read this account that there was something quite ancient and even pagan about it.

The very last line of the narrative tells us that St Matthew died on 16 November, and this is still his feast day as far as the Eastern Church is concerned, though as far back as the 6th century St Matthew's feast day in the West has been 21 September. As we have pointed out frequently, this date marks the autumn equinox – a date that would have had supreme significance to worshippers of Mithras. It is also worth reiterating that Charles-François Dupuis observed that in Persian mythology Mithras was crucified on 22 March, at the spring equinox.

There could be many more parallels between the story of St Matthew at Myrna and the legends of Mithras. Unfortunately, we will almost certainly never know because the Christian Church made such a good job of eradicating all traces of Mithraism in its pure form.

The Apprentice Pillar and Mithras

Turning our attention towards the Chapel itself, we can now see that the so-called Apprentice Pillar, in addition to representing the tree summoned up by St Matthew at Myrna, also represents the birth of Mithras. For all we know, Mithras himself may have been responsible for such a world tree when he fired his arrow at the rock. In addition, the fruits of the earth were closely associated with Mithras and formed part of the ritual meals that were eaten in the mithraeum, which was where celebrants of Mithras met.

What we don't find in Rosslyn Chapel is any representation of the bull-slaying scene that is so common as an association with Mithras. This is hardly surprising because learned visitors, especially from Rome, might have been familiar with the scene and would have known instantly what such iconography meant. However, it should also be remembered that the bull-slaying scene of Mithraism dealt with circumstances that were appropriate in the centuries approaching the modern era – in other words, before AD 1. In the years following the appearance of Mithraism in the West, the spring equinox, which had been in Aries, passed into the sign of Pisces. As

8. Photograph of Agnus Dei from Piece Hall, Halifax, Yorkshire

a result, the sacrificial victim from that point on would not be the bull but rather the ram or sheep of the zodiac sign of Aries. All of this coincides very nicely with the appearance of a symbol, both inside and outside of the Church, that was to become synonymous with the Faith. That symbol is the Lamb of God or, in Latin, the Agnus Dei.

A typical representation of the Agnus Dei can be seen in this picture. It comes from the entrance to the Piece Hall in Halifax, Yorkshire, England and in this instance is associated with the head of John the Baptist. In very early examples of the Agnus Dei, the lamb is often shown with its feet tied together because it is meant to represent a sacrificial victim.

The lamb or sheep as a sacrificial victim begins to appear regularly in a religious connotation around the time of the appearance of Christianity. In particular, it has become attached to Christianity, though it previously held an important part in Judaism, in association with the feast of Passover. Jesus himself is regularly referred to in the New Testament of the Bible, and especially in the Book of Revelation, as the 'Lamb of God', and a prayer associated with the Catholic Mass begins 'Lamb of God who takes away the sins of the world ...'

The Jewish Passover was celebrated around the time of the spring equinox, and it was with this celebration in mind that Christianity fixed the calculation that leads to the date of Easter, which of course commemorates the crucifixion of Jesus. It seems certain that this is connected to the fact that around AD 1, the spring equinox began to occur not in Aries, as it had done, but in the sign of Pisces – in other words, the ram or lamb was sacrificed, as had been the bull before it.

The Christian Church, in representing Jesus as the sacrificed lamb, would therefore have been playing directly into the hands of Mithraists, whose expertise in astronomy would have told them that from the start of the modern era Mithras would not kill a bull but rather a sheep. As with most Christian churches there are representations of the Agnus Dei in Rosslyn Chapel, but the symbol of the lamb is also an important part of Freemasonry.

An indispensable component of every Freemasonic ritual is the clothing worn by those present at such ceremonies. The most significant part of this attire is an apron, which is almost invariably made from sheepskin or the skin of a lamb. Freemasons are told that this symbolizes purity, but Robert Hewitt Brown is emphatic that it actually represents the spring equinox and the sign of Aries.[4]

It is also worth mentioning briefly that Freemasonry does not concern itself solely with matters associated with the Sun. At its core the Craft pays almost as much attention to the planet Venus, which ranks high in terms of Freemasonic symbolism. Freemasonry is the legatee of a mystery religion and, as such, concerns itself with the *feminine* as much as it does with the *masculine*. As I demonstrated, particularly in my book *Washington DC – City of the Goddess*,[5] much Freemasonic attention is focussed not only on Venus but also on the zodiac sign of Virgo, which itself is relevant to the autumn equinox and to harvest time. Many mystery religions such as those of Demeter and Isis dealt specifically with the union of God and Goddess, and it is quite likely that Mithraism also worked in this way. Some slight evidence does remain because the second degree of Mithraism was known as the Male Bride and was dedicated specifically to Venus.

The Crypt as a Temple

The connections between Mithraism, Freemasonry and Rosslyn Chapel are beginning to mount up, but now we need to look at the actual building itself because there are other ways in which it displays its Mithraic associations.

Many mithraea have been discovered across the Roman world. They tend to have survived better than normal temples, partly because they were often underground structures. We know that they were not especially large and always had barrel-vaulted roofs in order to resemble the cave where Mithras and Helios consumed the bull, which, in turn, represented the cosmos.

We have always been fascinated by the crypt or lower chapel at Rosslyn. It is approached by a flight of steep stairs from the southern side of the east end of the Chapel. What makes it different from normal crypts is that there is no evidence that anyone was buried there, which is common practice in most churches. The room is generally devoid of extensive ornamentation and is certainly not as lavishly decorated as the Chapel itself. Any paintings that may have once existed on the walls have long since disappeared, but it does retain its barrel-vaulted roof.

The lower chapel at Rosslyn would also qualify as a mithraeum by dint of its orientation. All mithraea were entered from the west and had their altars in the east. The only things missing from the lower chapel, in order to make it into an instant and typical mithraeum, are the benches, upon which those present rested and the various altars dedicated to Mithras. Again, the absence of the latter is hardly surprising, since the building could be visited and inspected at any time by Church dignitaries.

As a result of all this, the notion that Rosslyn Chapel was once the site of a mithraeum is not as far-fetched as it might at first have appeared. We have always taken the suggestion to mean that centuries *prior* to the building of the Chapel there had been a mithraeum on the site, in other words one of Roman date, but if a form of Mithraism survived in Scotland this need not have been the case. Suggestions have been made (strong enough to be mentioned in an article written for the BBC and posted online) that the lower chapel, which is also sometimes known as the sacristy, is older than the upper chapel. Some say the original Rosslyn Castle was situated on this site and that the lower chapel is part of this structure, but as far as we are aware there is no definitive proof that the Castle was moved.

When assessing the possibility of a mithraeum having existed on the site we cannot of course dismiss the main Chapel itself. Although somewhat larger than mithraea seem to have been, it too has many of the credentials. Bearing in mind that the original cave of Mithraism represented the cosmos, the builders of Rosslyn Chapel thoughtfully placed stars all over the inside of the barrel-vaulted roof to bear testimony to the Chapel itself being a representation of the cosmos.

We always believed that, on a balance of probabilities, Freemasonry came into existence in a formalized sense at Rosslyn Chapel. Like other researchers we considered it likely that the original Sir William Sinclair had wished to keep aspects of the Chapel's *real* symbolism, and even purpose, a closely guarded secret. This could have been the case for a variety of reasons – especially if the head of St Matthew had been present. As a result we suggested that Freemasonry represented a way for Earl William to bring all his workers together in a tightly knit fraternity, based on supposed archaic secrets and buttressed by horrible oaths of torture and death for anyone who disclosed the secrets. While this seemed to be a reasonable explanation, in some respects it lacked substance. It might have been the reason that developing Freemasonry was associated with architecture and building, but it would not explain the cosmological heart of the Craft.

It cannot be denied that a surviving form of Mithraism may be a better explanation for the rise and development of Freemasonry. As we have demonstrated, Earl William Sinclair and Sir Gilbert Haye were both learned individuals and they possessed an extensive library that included works on philosophy, religion, history, alchemy, astronomy and a host of other subjects. They had all the information they needed to make Mithraism, or something like it, into a fraternal association, apparently based on architecture and stonemasonry, but in reality disguising something truly archaic and at the same time deeply religious. On the other hand, Freemasonry may have already existed in this form prior to the planning and building of the Chapel – in which case we see on the site a structure that was created, in part at least, to allow this fraternity to flourish and grow.

Is it possible that Mithraism, or something closely associated with it, could have survived the long period between the 5th or 6th centuries and the 15th century? Many people will say no, but if they do, they are allowing their own prejudices to obscure what is quite provable evidence. Almost all researchers agree, as would anyone who looked at the subject deeply enough, that Freemasonry is based on astronomy – and what is more, astronomy with a strong religious content.

Hewitt Brown suggested that the figure of adoration was the Sun itself, but this does not appear to be the case. He knew little or nothing about Mithraism and did not deal at all with the significance of the precession of the equinoxes to developing religion around the start of the modern era.[6]

Freemasonry was never quite, as Hewitt Brown suggested, obsessed with worship of the Sun because at the heart of the Craft is that mysterious but all-important character known as 'the Grand Architect of the Universe'. In other words, the religious presence at the heart of Freemasonry stands *above and beyond* a celestial body such as the Sun. The term sounds much more like that attributed to a deity with sufficient power to *move* the universe, and that character is Mithras, with his equinox-shifting abilities.

Be that as it may, the very fact that Freemasonry still exists and is so popular across the world proves conclusively that ancient beliefs can and do survive, nested within society and surviving despite the efforts of so many agencies to destroy them. Whether or not all or even any of those practising Freemasonry are fully aware of what they are doing is quite beside the point. In reality, the fact that, in the main, members *do not* know what lies at the core of Freemasonry could be part of the reason it managed to survive.

Over the years Freemasonry has offered brotherhood and a classless environment in class-ridden societies. It has been a self-help group amongst its members and has supported them and their families in times of hardship. Freemasonry is broadly equivalent to the coming-of-age ceremonies that all men, and probably women, too, once experienced in tribal societies, and in this it probably serves a psychological need. Freemasonry offers a *commonality* and a point of reference in a changeable and often frightening world. In other words, to many individuals Freemasonry has been important on a number of different levels – none of which were necessarily related to religious belief.

What a supremely clever and forward-looking strategy this has been. It is a little like discovering the amazing medicinal properties of a particular plant, but encouraging gardeners to grow it for its rapturous perfume and glorious blossoms. When it comes to curing the sick, the potency of the plant remains, even though the majority of those who cultivate it know nothing of this. Only those who *really* investigate its potential will ever be party to the truth.

CHAPTER TWELVE

The View to the West

At the time Rosslyn Chapel was built, Scotland was a very different country to the one that existed only two or three centuries later. It was fully independent, self-assured and, as we have seen, often at odds with its larger but no more illustrious southern neighbour, England. Scotland successfully conducted its own affairs, passed its own laws and took its place as a full sovereign state within the Western European family of nations. It was probably assumed by William Sinclair and his family that Scotland would always retain its independence and its viability as an independent kingdom, but, thanks once again to the influence of England, this would not be the case. In the end, much of the best that Scotland could offer ended up far from the shores of Britain – and this may have included at least some of what had lain in secret for centuries beneath Rosslyn Chapel.

Scotland is not a particularly populous country. At present, only around six million people live north of the border, whereas in England an estimated eight million people live in

Greater London alone. When the vast area of Scotland is taken into account, this shows that there are far less individuals per square kilometre in Scotland than is the case in England. There are a number of reasons for this state of affairs and part of the situation is a legacy of history.

By the 18th century much of the land in Scotland was owned by either absent English landlords or by clan chiefs, many of whom were being educated in England and probably resided there, too. Most of these landowners were hungry for money, and they did not see the peppercorn rents paid by crofters and villagers on their land as representing a good income. Tenants needed to be looked after in various ways; rent had to be collected, and land management for subsistence farming could be quite expensive. Meanwhile, aristocrats had learned a valuable lesson from the monastic orders that flourished in Britain from the 12th century until the 16th century and that lesson was that it is much cheaper and more profitable to keep sheep than it is to have small-scale tenant farmers on one's land.

As a result, at first in England, but then to a much greater extent in Scotland, landowners sought to move tenants off their land in order to create large areas in which sheep could be grazed. Sheep do not need a great deal of attention, can live on poor vegetation and offer cash crops, in terms of wool, skins and meat. It seemed like common sense to everyone, except of course to the tenants. They were often moved to villages on the coast and told to become fishermen or were encouraged to leave Scotland altogether, to travel to the Colonies in North America, Australia or New Zealand.

Tens of thousands of Scots men, women and children were forced from the land of their birth and were obliged to make homes and lives for themselves far away from home. Being the resilient people they were, many prospered and flourished, but Scotland itself never really recovered from the depletion of its population and is still significantly underpopulated at the start of the 21st century.

With the arrival of the Industrial Revolution in Great Britain, Scotland began to produce far more than its fair share of engineers. We saw earlier in the book how the education system, and particularly the universities of Scotland, fostered a greater ability for working-class children to gain an advanced education than was the case in England. The result was some of the finest engineering brains available, especially during the late 18th and the 19th century. Many of these individuals followed the general trend for Scots to seek employment either in England or, just as likely, far from home. Another resort for young Scottish men was the armed forces. Those joining the army or navy did not necessarily require an extensive education; they would get to travel, and though the wages would not have been good, they were are least guaranteed. In the 18th century especially, this meant that many Scots soldiers would find themselves stationed in Britain's North American Colonies, which did not gain their independence until the 1780s.

New Worlds for Old

By the middle of the 18th century, Freemasonry was growing apace and nowhere more so than in Scotland, the place of its origin. Freemasonry was also extremely popular within the armed forces. As a result, British and especially Scot's settlers took their Freemasonry with them to the New World; many of the Scottish soldiers garrisoned there were also Freemasons and belonged to Regimental Lodges.

It has been suggested, and to a great extent proved, by the writers Leigh and Baigent in their book *The Temple and the Lodge*[1] that Freemasonry had a great part to play in the struggle of the British Colonies in North America to gain their independence. Many of the American freedom fighters were attached to companies and ultimately regiments that had been formed from specific Freemasonic lodges throughout the Colonies. Indeed, the very origins of the American settlers' break with Britain is traceable, in no small measure, to Freemasons from specific lodges, especially in Boston, Massachusetts. Highlanders and members of their families that survived the Battle of Culloden in the 18th century were offered initiation into the Craft, and four guineas if they joined the British army and agreed to fight against the Revolutionary Colonists in the War of Independence. This seemed like a way out of poverty and persecution for many of the clansmen, but there was no love lost in the deal.

Although there have only ever been three degrees in Craft Freemasonry, America provided a hotbed for the development of other Masonic bodies, which allowed Freemasons to explore extra degrees. Contemporary with the search for American freedom, new associations such as York Rite Freemasonry and Scottish Rite Freemasonry began to develop. York Rite claimed to have its origins in England, whereas Scottish Rite, in its original form, developed in France, from previous Scottish advanced degrees. It came to the United States via the West Indies and then New Orleans, before appearing in New York and then spreading across all the states.

The American War of Independence began in 1775, and some of the avenues for achieving high degrees in Freemasonry were already available in the Colonies at this time. It is true that Scottish Rite, as it is known today, had not yet come fully into being, but the bodies and degrees from which it developed were present and would have been well known to many of those who first proposed the American Colonial divorce from Great Britain.

Many of the Revolutionary leaders in America were enthusiastic Freemasons – the most famous of whom was George Washington and it may have been, in part, his and his compatriots' Freemasonic leanings that led them to break away from Britain. There is no absolute proof that another, and possibly the most important of the founding fathers of the Revolution, Thomas Jefferson, was a Freemason, but everything about his life, his beliefs and his actions tends to indicate that he was. At the very least he was extremely familiar with Masonic ideals, and he also had a good understanding of the history of Britain, including Scotland. He was responsible for trying to recruit the dispossessed Stewart claimant to the British throne, Prince Charles Edward Stewart, to become King of the Revolutionary Colonists and even travelled to Rome to meet him, although by this time Charles was not a well man, a poor shadow of his former self, ruined by disappointment and alcohol. Was it because of his position as the shadowy superior in Jacobite Freemasonry that the Colonists wanted Charles Stewart? This we will never know.

It was Thomas Jefferson who first wrote the words of the American Declaration of Independence which, in 1776, set out the reasons why the North American Colonies had decided that a break with Great Britain was inevitable. There are striking parallels between the American Declaration of Independence and the much earlier Scottish Declaration of Arbroath (mentioned in detail in Chapter Five). It has been suggested that the Declaration of Arbroath was Jefferson's template when he created America's own document.

Together with Christopher Knight, Alan has researched and written comprehensively on the importance of Freemasonry to the United States of America. Alan's book, *Before the Pyramids*,[2] co-authored with Christopher Knight, and his later book, *City of the Goddess*,[3] both give an in-depth account of the part Freemasonry played in the building of the United States, and especially the founding of its capital city in Washington DC.

Freemasonry, and particularly Scottish Rite Freemasonry, was, and to a great extent still is, of the greatest importance in the founding and development of Washington DC, and testaments to the Craft's presence can be found all over the city. Probably the earliest and most significant legacy of Freemasonry is the United States Capitol – the building in which all US government business is thrashed out – in other words, the political and democratic heart of the nation. The position of the Capitol, on a significant hill to the east of a long, green avenue known as the Mall was already decided upon when the first designs of the prospective city were made. This job was undertaken by Pierre Charles L'Enfant (1754–1825), a French architect, freedom fighter and noted Freemason. Nobody has the slightest doubt that Freemasonry with its aims, objectives and symbolism was in the mind of L'Enfant when he produced the first plans of Washington DC.

The Cornerstone of the Capitol

The foundation stone of the Capitol was laid with a great Freemasonic ceremony on 18 September 1793. The cornerstone was laid by George Washington himself, dressed in full Masonic regalia and attended by at least three separate Masonic lodges. Even the date is significant because it is close to the pivotal autumn equinox that has figured so heavily in our story so far. From an astronomical perspective (and we have seen how important astronomy is to Freemasonry) the day in question was especially significant. The first of the planets to rise that morning in the east was Venus. She stood bright and brilliant as a morning star, having cut the horizon at 3.30am. She was soon followed by Mars, and then the recently discovered Uranus. Mercury followed, bright and beautiful, a full hour before the Sun at 5.50am and then finally, at 6.30 the Sun itself appeared. Perhaps most important of all, the Sun occupied the zodiac sign of Virgo, which has always been of supreme importance to Freemasonry and which seems to have been of significance to Mithraism also. The Sun was less than a degree away from the position of the autumn equinox.

All of this accords incredibly well with what the sky looked like on St Matthew's day, 1456, when it seems certain the cornerstone of Rosslyn Chapel was laid in far-off Scotland.

Six years earlier, on 17 September 1787, the Constitution of the new United States of America had been signed, under very similar astronomical portents, with both Mercury and Venus rising before the Sun, with the Sun in the zodiac sign of Virgo and almost touching the point of autumn equinox. In both examples these dates were clearly not chosen arbitrarily. In the case of the signing of the Constitution, the delegates had been present in Philadelphia for many weeks and seem to have delib-erately delayed the final signing for some unspecified reason – which, in fact, was clearly a case of waiting until the astro-nomical and astrological circumstances were *just right* to offer the new Constitution all the assistance the sky could afford.[4]

The Capitol itself was always intended to be a magnifi-cent building. It had a prime position, on a hill and, with its double-fronted configuration, facing due east and due west. The Capitol is, like Rosslyn Chapel, a natural astronomical observatory. The external balconies of its round dome give an unrestricted view of the sky across 360°, and from the day it was planned, right up until now, no building in Washington DC (except the Washington Monument, which also has important astronomical overtones) has ever been allowed to be higher than the Capitol.

The Capitol looks like a Greek temple, which is no accident. Although it is true that classical architecture was all the rage when the various stages of the Capitol were undertaken, it is, in reality a temple – in this case, a temple to Liberty. Liberty is more than an ideal, she was also a Roman goddess, who was particularly venerated by freed slaves. (Like Mithras she wore the Phrygian cap – the cap of freedom.) In the United States she was eventually renamed Columbia, and her form can be seen all over the city. Most significant of all, and in this case called Armed Freedom, she stands six metres tall on the very pinnacle of the dome of the Capitol and she faces east, towards the rising Sun.[5]

None of this symbolism is remotely accidental. The whole city of Washington is dedicated to this goddess, the proof of which is that the area within which Washington stands is called the District of Columbia. Columbia is the hidden goddess at the very heart of Freemasonry and, as Venus, would have represented the consort of Mithras.

It has been suggested by many researchers that those planning the Capitol were also emulating the Temple of Solomon in Jerusalem, which likewise stood atop a hill, with the window in the Holy of Holies looking out to the east. This would be particularly appropriate to Freemasons, who, as we have seen, have a special reverence for Solomon's Temple. And so if the Temple in Jerusalem was conceived as a temple to the Sun, then so was the Capitol.

It was demonstrated in Alan's books *Before the Pyramids* and *City of the Goddess* that when the plans for Washington DC were first laid down, the unit of measurement that was used was an extremely ancient one. This is known as the Megalithic Yard, and it was the standard unit of linear measurement used in the construction of most of the Neolithic henges, stone circles and stone avenues built between around 3500 BC and 1500 BC in Britain and large parts of France. This, together with a geometric unit based upon the polar circumference of the Earth and equalling 366 Megalithic Yards, underpins all of Washington DC. It creates an apparently hidden but very potent *matrix* upon which most of the important buildings in Washington DC, and practically all its major intersections, were based. Interestingly, this Megalithic matrix was never forgotten by some of the powerbrokers of Washington DC because as recently as the 1980s it was still employed in the placement of significant civic structures such as the World War II Memorial on the Mall.[6]

Imagine our surprise when, some years ago, we discovered that an area of Washington DC, just across the Potomac River to the west of the centre of the city, is named Rosslyn. This seemed slightly odd to us because by the time *anyone* was travelling from Britain to the New World, the village where Rosslyn Chapel stands was already known as *Roslin,* and had been for centuries. In other words, apart from the Chapel and the Castle, there is no place called Rosslyn. This meant that the district in question must have been named after the location of the Chapel and Castle, and not after the village.

It has proved to be impossible for us to discover why this area of Washington DC was so named. These days it is an area of high-rise office blocks and apartments, but historically it was, especially during the 19th century, a fairly run-down sort of district, filled with drinking houses. Some researchers put the name of the district down to the fact that there had once been a farm there owned by William and Carolyn Ross, and that the name had originally been Ross Lynn, though it has been hard to substantiate the truth of this assertion which, as is so often the case in these matters, could easily be a deliberately created red herring. Many years ago when John was a member of the Friends of Rosslyn management team, he built a website called Rosslyn.com; this dates back to 1992 and it was exceptionally busy for that period. However, one of its crossed wires was that it used to receive technical emails of a military nature. After sending back emails for several weeks, they eventually stopped. Later, John discovered that Rosslyn was indeed part of the American Intelligence Network – a fact that was not generally known. Luckily nothing of import was revealed.

The Cathedral of St Matthew

The existence of an area of Washington DC with this name caused us to look deeper at the possible connections between Washington DC and Rosslyn Chapel. Washington DC has two cathedrals. Washington National Cathedral is located at Wisconsin Avenue and was commenced in 1907. It is a Protestant, Episcopal foundation and is dedicated to St Peter and St Paul. Washington DC's second cathedral is Roman Catholic. It began as a Catholic church, on the corner of 15th and H Streets, in 1840. In 1892, land was purchased for the present site, which is on Rhode Island Avenue, and the Cathedral's first Mass was celebrated in 1895. This is the older of the two cathedrals in the city and is dedicated to St Matthew!

Why did a Cathedral in Washington DC come to be dedicated to St Matthew? The history section of the Cathedral website suggests that the dedication is due to the fact that St Matthew is known as the patron saint of civil servants, of which naturally there are many in Washington DC. At the same time it cannot be denied that Washington DC is a city planned and built by Freemasons, and upon Freemasonic symbolism. Since Guild Freemasonry almost certainly had early beginnings at Rosslyn Chapel, and because Rosslyn Chapel is dedicated to St Matthew, it seems likely that there is a connection. True, Roman Catholicism has often been critical of Freemasonry, but that has not prevented many Roman Catholics from also being members of lodges. Nor should it be forgotten that Rosslyn Chapel also started its life, nominally at least, as a Roman Catholic foundation.

The most likely and certainly the most fascinating connection between Rosslyn Chapel and Washington DC involves an intriguing story of treasure, a medieval order of fighting monks called the Knights Templar and the continuation of a legacy going back in time at least 3,000 years and possibly longer.

Rosslyn Chapel and the Knights Templar

In order to understand the connection we must first acknowledge the belief, widely held by researchers into Rosslyn Chapel, that it not only has an association with Freemasonry but also with the Knights Templar. The Templars were founded officially in 1129, when Pope Honorius II hosted a Church Council in the city of Troyes, Champagne, France. Some years prior to this, in 1119, a Troyes nobleman by the name of Hugues de Payens, who had previously fought in the First Crusade and had been present at the fall of Jerusalem to the Christians in 1099, returned to the Holy City. He took with him eight other knights (mostly relatives) and declared his objective to be the protection of Christian pilgrims on the road from the Mediterranean coast to Jerusalem. The little band was promptly adopted by the Christian King of Jerusalem, Baldwin II, who gave them lodgings in stables, in a place on the Temple Mount, where the Temple of Jerusalem had once stood.

At this point, the band of knights disappear from history until 1129, when they turned up in Troyes and were granted the right to become Holy Knights, fighting for Christendom. They were to be called The Poor Fellow-Soliders of Christ and of the Temple of Solomon and would fall under the direct jurisdiction of the pope himself. In reality, they had not simply come to Troyes speculatively. They had a patron – a very influential man by the name of Bernard of Clairvaux. Bernard was one of the leading lights of the fairly new Cistercian monastic order, and during his time in the order he had become highly placed in the Church of his day. He was, in effect, a pope-maker, and Honorius II and at least two other popes greatly owed their positions to his influence.

No reasonable request coming from the direction of Bernard of Clairvaux would have been refused by Honorius, and in any case he was pleased enough to have professional Christian soldiers fighting in the East on behalf of the Church. Once the order was established, the Templars grew from the original nine members to being fantastically successful. They acquired land and grants of money from all over Europe and beyond, and ultimately became much more than holy warriors. In a short space of time the Templars became shippers, farmers, bankers, tax collectors and power brokers on a massive scale; they held the crowned heads of many states in Europe in their palms.

The story of the Templars is a long and involved one, but suffice it to say that they prospered until 1307, when the King of France, Philip IV, decided that he and the rest of Europe could get on much better without them. This is mostly because the Templars owned half his kingdom in loans and also because the order was so powerful it was feared that at any moment the Templars may decide to set up their own state, probably in the south of France, in Philip's back yard.

On 13 October 1307, every Templar establishment in France was raided by forces loyal to Philip IV and all the Templars found were arrested. Philip was able to take these steps because at the time he 'owned' the papacy, in the form of Pope Clement V, who Philip had arranged to be elected pope and who was stationed not in Rome but in French Avignon. The Templars were accused of a long list of heresies against the Church, including denying Christ, perverting the Mass, spitting on the Crucifix and taking part in ceremonies that were not authorized by the Church.

The verdict was never in doubt. The Grand Master of the Templars, Jacques de Molay, was eventually burned alive in Paris in 1314, and the order was officially disbanded.

The Treasures of Jerusalem

If ever there was a subject that has fascinated conspiracy theorists more than any other, it is that of the Knights Templar. To some researchers they were peerless white knights who genuinely worked for God, whilst to others they were self-seeking, arrogant materialists who virtually engineered their own demise as a result of their greed and power-hungry actions. In the middle are those historians who recognize that there were points for and against the Templars, and that the reasons for their downfall were many and complex.

The part of the Templar story that particularly interests us is the period of time they spent in Jerusalem between 1119 and 1129, when they were supposed to be guarding the roads between Jerusalem and the Mediterranean ports – a task some said was achieved by diplomatic means. There is no mention in history of them doing anything physical of the sort, and it is accepted, especially in Freemasonic circles, that they were, in reality, excavating below the Temple mound under their garrison, over the ruins of Solomon's Temple. Freemasonic stories suggest that they were looking for something specific and also assert that they found it – though what this might have been remains a mystery.

As is often the case with Freemasonry, if one looks deep enough into the Craft's stories and symbolism, answers are often forthcoming. In this case we need to look at the ceremonies attached to the Royal Arch degrees. There we are told a story about events that took place before the founding of the Temple of Solomon. The story tells of a group of men who excavated on Mount Moriah (where the Temple was built) prior to or during the planning of Solomon's Temple. There they found ruins, and after breaking through a number of stone arches they came to a chamber in which was a gold plaque, known as a delta of Enoch, on which was inscribed the sacred and secret name of God.

The finding of the chamber and the Delta of Enoch is recalled in great detail in Masonic ritual and is told as a first-hand account. Because of the ultimate connections between Freemasonry and the Templars, it began to be suggested that this story was probably more than a myth and that it paraphrased the *real* excavation that took place on the Temple Mount in the 12th century. As a result, it eventually became more or less accepted that the first Templars had indeed been searching for something specific in Jerusalem and that whatever they had found was ultimately brought back to France.

Some writers speculated that the Templars had discovered the Ark of the Covenant, the gold-covered wooden box that once stood in the Holy of Holies in the Temple. The story became linked with carvings at the Cathedral of Chartres, which show knights apparently bringing an ark to the building. As a result, an assumption was made that Chartres Cathedral, which some thought had been financed and even built by the Templars, had been intended as the resting place of the Ark – or whatever treasures the Templars had actually found.

If we assume for a moment that the first Templar knights had indeed spent part or all of the missing ten years digging on the Temple Mount, and that they had discovered something of importance in the many tunnels and chambers that are known to have existed in the three successive Temples that occupied the same location, what is the likelihood that what they discovered would end up in Chartres? First of all, the chance of the discovery having been the Ark of the Covenant is surely just too far-fetched to be taken seriously? The Ark is mentioned a great deal in the Old Testament of the Bible, but even if it had survived the various ravages of time and the destruction of Solomon's Temple and its successors, it would most surely have fallen into Roman hands when the most recent Temple was destroyed in AD 70. In any case, the Ark is not mentioned at all in the Masonic rituals that seem to play out the story of the Templar excavations.

If anything had been found by the Templars, would they have brought it back to Chartres? Again, this seems unlikely. The present Cathedral of Chartres was not commenced until 1193, over six decades after the Templars returned from Jerusalem.

A far more likely destination for anything the first Templars discovered in Jerusalem would have been Troyes in Champagne. Troyes was the city in which the Templar order was founded, and the Count of Champagne became its first member after the Council of Troyes, which of course was also held in the city and which made the Templars into an official order. Although, in time, the Templars were represented in most of the major capitals of Western Europe and beyond, Troyes remained the order's first and most important base – as much as anything because the Templars were part of a strategy employed by the rulers of Champagne to bring trade and prosperity to their region.

The whole situation changed just before the demise of the Templars, when the region of Champagne came into the hands of the French Crown. This came about as a result of some astute political manoeuvring by the father of King Philip IV, who had his son betrothed to the surviving heiress of Champagne, Joan of Navarre. Joan died in 1305, just two years before her husband Philip IV moved against the Templars. Those ruling the Templar order were shrewd. They could not have failed to know that Philip IV hated the order and they were aware that he was avaricious, scheming and cruel. From the moment when Joan of Navarre died, it was only a matter of time before Champagne would be lost, and it is certain that the Templars would have moved any treasures away from the city of Troyes and from the region of Champagne in advance of their demise – which was clearly expected.

Nowhere in France would have been safe. What the Templars needed was a location well away from the machinations of Philip IV or his tame pope. The obvious choice would have been Scotland. Early in 1306, Robert the Bruce, who would soon become King of the Scots, had been excommunicated by the pope, as a result of the murder of a man called John Comyn before the altar in Greyfriars church in Dumfries. It was not *who* the murdered man was that inspired the pope's wrath, but *where* it was done, because the sanctuary of the church had been breached. Not only Bruce himself suffered, but the whole of Scotland had also been effectively excommunicated.

After the middle of 1306, Scotland was temporarily beyond the influence of the papacy. At the same time, Robert the Bruce was fighting ferociously against the English, who, as always, were attempting to exert their influence over Scotland. Bruce needed all the support he could get.

In 1314, a decisive battle took place between the Scots and the English. The battle was fought at Bannockburn and the forces of the English were routed. It was probably the greatest victory the Scots ever had over the English, other than the battle of Rosslyn in 1303. Popular legends, developing soon after the battle, suggest that white-mantled knights, believed to be Templars, had fought for Bruce during his decisive victory.

Since the Templars had been pronounced heretical by the pope himself, all kings of Catholic countries were expected to arrest and try Templars in their domains. By 1309, King Robert the Bruce was back in the Catholic fold, but trials of Templars in Scotland were not pursued with any great enthusiasm. There certainly was a Templar presence in Scotland, and, what is more, it predated the official sanctioning of the order in 1129.

Hugues de Payens visited Scotland in 1128. There is a suggestion that he was, or had been, married to an heiress of the St Clairs, whose name was Catherine or Katherine. Whether this is true or not, King David I definitely did meet Hugues de Payens in Scotland in June 1128 and granted to him the lands of Balantrodoch, not far from Edinburgh. The site is now the location of a village that is known to this day as Temple. The village of Temple lies only four miles east of Rosslyn, across two valleys.

Many writers have suggested that whatever treasure or artefacts the Templars originally found in Jerusalem, after residing for a couple of centuries in France, was eventually buried below Rosslyn Chapel – which, it has been suggested, was built specifically for that purpose. Rosslyn Chapel as we know it today did not of course exist at this time, but Rosslyn Castle certainly did.

If indeed there was any such treasure, when first arriving in Scotland, it may have been deposited in one of the abbeys of the Tironensian monks, discussed in Chapter Five. The most likely contender would seem to be the Abbey of Kilwinning, which, as we have seen, is a strong contender for the start of Freemasonry and is closely associated with the later Rosslyn Chapel.

Writing with Christopher Knight in *Before the Pyramids*, Alan speculated that this same treasure could easily have been removed from below Rosslyn Chapel at the middle of the 19th century, when extensive repairs were being undertaken, if they knew where the entrance to the chamber was! As we saw much earlier, Queen Victoria had shown an interest in Rosslyn Chapel and suggested that it should be preserved. This was a time when the United States of America was beginning to show itself as potentially one of the greatest nations on the planet. It was also a period during which Scottish Rite Freemasonry was beginning to gain a strong foothold in the United States – a form of Freemasonry which, as its name implies, was thought to have first developed in Scotland.

In *Before the Pyramids* the suggestion is that the Delta of Enoch and the Book of Abel first of all found their way to the area of Washington DC known to this day as Rosslyn, where, when circumstances allowed, they were buried with due ceremony but in absolute secrecy at the very centre of the District of Columbia, right in the heart of Washington

DC. The chamber where it rests, together with ancient scrolls and documents also collected by the Knights Templar, lies below the centre of a park known as Ellipse Park, which is itself immediately to the south of the White House. We refer readers who are interested in this possibility to *Before the Pyramids*.

A Recreation of Solomon's Temple

Undoubtedly, there is a strong emotional connection between Freemasons in the United States of America and Rosslyn Chapel. On an almost daily basis, American Masons arrive at the Chapel, where both of us have talked to many of them, as well as taking part in numerous television documentaries about Rosslyn Chapel, specifically for American consumption.

According to Christopher Knight and Robert Lomas in their best-selling book *The Hiram Key*, Rosslyn Chapel is a deliberately created copy of what its builders considered Solomon's Temple would have looked like. Since there are also strong connections between the theoretical Solomon's Temple and the Capitol in Washington DC, a direct connection between Rosslyn Chapel and the Capitol is also evident.

The flame of freedom and liberty, which has always been of great significance to the Scots, burns brightly in the United States, and the Freemasonry that doubtless began in something like its present form in Rosslyn Chapel is not only evident across Washington DC but throughout the United States – a fitting connection between this truly wondrous Gothic masterpiece and the most powerful nation on Earth.

CHAPTER THIRTEEN

The Judaic Connections

W hen we decided to write this book, it seemed appropriate to entitle it *Rosslyn Chapel Decoded*. We have always believed, and remain certain of the fact, that Rosslyn Chapel cannot be looked at 'straight on'. It becomes ever clearer to us that it was always the intention of Earl William Sinclair and Sir Gilbert Haye to incorporate the *synthesis* of their combined knowledge into this remarkable little building. As a result, we felt it was appropriate to take a journey into the medieval mind, as well as into the personal library of the Sinclairs, to try and view the many levels of acquired knowledge that contributed to a finished product that, nearly six centuries later, still keeps its lonely vigil above the Glen.

As we have seen, there can be little doubt that the planners of Rosslyn Chapel were expert astronomers. Nor can we doubt that they were men who had been deeply influenced not only by the material that was available to them but also their own upbringings, their position in space and time, and also the many traditions that were endemic to this unique place, some of which feel nearly as old as the stone from which the Chapel was constructed. It is highly likely that knowledge of the old mystery religions, together with the strong Culdean influence that still pervaded Scottish Christianity even in the 15th century, played a part in the Chapel's planning. In addition, there are so many connections between the cosmology that lay at the heart of Mithraism and the reality of the Chapel's own credentials as an astronomical observatory that even this connection is a real possibility, and more so bearing in mind the Freemasonic connections the Chapel has always maintained. We should not ignore the aspects of many other world religions that are represented in Rosslyn both in the carvings and philosophic symbolism.

All the same, we should never ignore the evidence of our own eyes and there are a couple of very strong skeins of visual evidence at Rosslyn Chapel with which we have not yet dealt; we felt it appropriate that these should come towards the end of our quest because in many ways they are the most intriguing. First of all, there are extremely strong connections between many of the carvings in Rosslyn Chapel and the oldest part of the Christian Bible – the Old Testament. The Old Testament cannot be considered a strictly Christian text, since all of it is also relevant to Judaism, the religion and culture from which Christianity sprang.

Wine is Strong

It is towards a series of specific events in the Old Testament that at least some of the best stone carving in Rosslyn Chapel

9. 'Wine is strong, a king is stronger, women are stronger still, but truth conquers all' – the only words, in Latin, carved into the stonework of Rosslyn Chapel

directs us. For example, we find a representation that may be that of the Persian King Darius. This identification seems likely because nearby we find the only words to be carved in stone at the Chapel. The phrase in question is in Latin and reads: '*Forte est vinum fortior est rex fortiores sunt mulieres super omnia vincit veritas*'; which can be translated into English as: 'Wine is strong, a king is stronger, women are stronger still, but truth conquers all.' This particular saying comes from the Old Testament of the Bible and is to be found in the Book of Esdras, which, although not included in the Catholic version of the Old Testament, is still considered to be authentic and from an ancient period. The saying carved into the east end of the Chapel appears in the account of a competition between three bodyguards of the Persian King Darius I, seeking to establish where in the world absolute strength lies. Various suggestions are made and explained, such as wine, a king and women, but Darius is the judge and awards victory to Zerubbabel, who is not a Persian but in fact a Hebrew. It is partly as a result of this competition that the Hebrews are released from captivity and allowed to return to Jerusalem to found a new Temple there.

The story is best illustrated by the historian Josephus, who claims it was King Darius, who released the Hebrews from bondage, though modern historians suggest this event took place under the rule of King Cyrus the Great, most likely around 551 BC. It is suggested elsewhere in the Bible that in the first year of his kingship, Cyrus had a revelation from God, which inspired him to release the Hebrews from captivity, to return to them all the gold and silver treasures that had formerly been stolen from the first Temple in Jerusalem and to instruct the building of a second Temple. Zerubbabel was one of the men charged with the job of rebuilding the Temple, a task that was duly undertaken. This story is also quoted as being part of a supposed conversation between Alexander the Great and his teacher Aristotle, as well as forming part of a story called *Alexander's Journey to Paradise*, a poem translated by Sir Gilbert Haye.

Even the story about the competition won by Zerubbabel has relevance to the feast day that is most potent to Rosslyn Chapel, which is that of St Matthew, on 21 September. The second Temple in Jerusalem was dedicated during the celebrations that took place in the month of Ethanim. These celebrations, the first of which was the Feast of Tabernacles, were timed to coincide with the autumn equinox, and so the Second Temple, and also in fact Solomon's first Temple, would both have been dedicated on or close to what would become St Matthew's Day.

It is partly the presence of these particular carvings within Rosslyn Chapel, together with others that are said to represent the celebrations that took place when the Second Temple was dedicated, that have led many authors (in particular Christopher Knight and Robert Lomas) to suggest that Rosslyn Chapel was deliberately intended to represent a version of the Hebrew Temple in Jerusalem. It cannot be denied that the pictographic evidence represented by the carvings in the east end of the Chapel, together with other considerations mentioned earlier in this book, such as the building's form, do seem to ascribe a relationship with the Jerusalem Temple in the minds of the Chapel's builders, whilst the common dates of dedication could also be a strong clue because we are certain that the cornerstone of Rosslyn Chapel was laid on St Matthew's Day.

However, as Alan showed with Christopher Knight in *Solomon's Powerbrokers*[1], there were some inevitable complications regarding the Jewish calendar, which was essentially lunar in nature. As a result, it cannot be absolutely reconciled with the modern calendar, which is solar-based. In the Jewish system, the month of Ethanim, which is now known as Tishri, can occur either in September or October, depending on the phases of the Moon in any given year. In other words, the Feast of the Tabernacles does not always coincide with the autumn equinox, a fact that annoyed one particular branch of Judaism that was extremely active around the time of the appearance of Christianity.

The sect in question was that of the Essenes. Much has been written about this fascinating offshoot of orthodox Judaism, and knowledge of it was strengthened by the discovery, in the 1940s, of a large cache of scrolls found in caves at Qumran, close to the River Jordan and not far from the Dead Sea.

These undoubted treasures had been hidden away in remote caves and began to reappear thanks to the efforts of local treasure hunters who learned that Western scholars in particular would pay handsomely for whole scrolls and even fragments found in the district. The whole collection of what are known to this day as the Dead Sea Scrolls was found between 1947 and 1956. They represent a veritable religious library, much of which relates to the Judaic Old Testament, though there are some texts previously unknown, and yet other works that were sometimes known to scholarship, but which had been lost in their original forms.

The finding of the Dead Sea Scrolls led to a significant increase in archaeology in the region, which, in turn, led to the discovery of the settlement in Qumran. It soon became associated with the Essenes, who appeared in the second century BC and who seem to have been present in the area in and around Jerusalem until not long after the life of Jesus. There is a great deal of evidence from studies by eminent professors who believe that Jesus went to school there from the age of 12, and it was the crucible of many Christian belief systems or cults. Although the Essenes were most definitely Jewish, there was much about them that differed from other forms of Judaism in that era. Not least of which was their reliance on a solar rather than a lunar calendar. Indeed, it has even been suggested that since the lunar calendar meant feast days and festivals were *not* always celebrated on the correct day of the year, this was part of what led the Essenes to split from their

Jewish cousins who followed different traditions.

The Essenes appear to have preferred life away from the hurly-burly and political intrigues of the large cities such as Jerusalem itself, and it has been suggested that sites such as Qumran were quasi-monastic settlements, most probably for men although women's graves contemporary with this date were found in the area. Qumran was established so that the Essenes could follow their own traditions and stick as closely as possible to what they considered to be the *word* of Jewish law.

According to the Jewish historian Josephus, in his works, *The Jewish War* (AD 79) and *Antiquities of the Jews* (AD 94), the Essenes represented a particular branch of Judaism, alongside the Pharisees and the Sadducees. He suggested that amongst their traditions they held piety to be of the utmost importance, together with celibacy and a policy of sharing all they had with the community as a whole. Josephus also points to certain practices of the Essenes that were dramatically different from any other branch of Judaism. In particular, he states that they took part in ritual bathing and that they devoted themselves totally to charity.

Essene Communities

The Essenes seem to have lived in communities that had much in common with later Christian monasticism, and they may have significantly affected individuals such as St Anthony the Great (c. AD 270) and others of the 'Desert Fathers', who took up residence in remote areas and lived the life of solitary hermits, or in small groups. The Desert Fathers, in turn, founded the idea of monasticism – taken up in particular by

St Benedict of Nursia (c. AD 480–547). It has been impossible to say with any certainty whether or not the Essenes, in their most austere form, created communities just for men. Certainly at Qumran burials of both men and women have been found – though it has to be remembered that females could be buried in Christian monasteries, but their presence did not mean that women formed part of the abbey communities. In reality it seems, according to Josephus, that there were two schools of Essenes: those who practised absolute chastity and those that allowed marriage – though only for the sake of procreation.

There is much about the ministry and teaching of Jesus, and also of his cousin John the Baptist, that betrays pure Essene influence, and there are many biblical scholars who suggest that Jesus actually *was* an Essene, or at the very least had studied at Qumran. Examples of Jesus' teaching that seem to point to Essene values include his instruction that his followers should give away what they possessed and live a life of poverty, and his particular concern for the poor, the sick and sinners. Many scholars also consider that John the Baptist was a member of the Qumran community and was in close contact with it in his role as a locum Essene, preaching in the region. According to the work of Dr Robert Feather, Jesus is said to have graduated from Qumran around the age of 30. According to the same researcher, St Matthew became a member of the Qumran community after the Crucifixion, but we believe he stayed there for over 12 years. He is said to have written most of his Gospel at Qumran, before he and the other disciples were instructed to go out into the world and spread the message, as demonstrated in the Gospel of St Matthew.*28:16–20.*

There are many people who believe that John the Baptist, and possibly even Jesus himself, was buried at Qumran. Certainly Dr Robert Feather in his book *The Secret Initiation of Jesus at Qumran*[2] lays out a great deal of evidence to support this hypothesis. This seems all the more likely when it is realized that Jesus as an Essene-Christian was often critical of the Pharisees and the Sadducees and their Sanhedrin.

Jesus' references to 'His Father's House', with the inference that following death, individuals would experience an afterlife, also accords with what Jospehus had to say about the beliefs of the Essenes – who appear to have premeditated the Christian concepts of heaven and hell.

The Essenes flourished during a period of great instability in terms of the Judaic homeland. By AD 70 there was a general Jewish uprising against the Romans, who ruled the entire area. Leading up to this event, many radical groups proliferated in and around Jerusalem, most notably the Zealots, who favoured armed rebellion in order to throw the Romans out of the area. It is not known whether the Zealots and the Essenes were closely associated, though in some ways it seems rather unlikely, since the Essenes were essentially peaceful, and, according to Josephus, although they were radical in a religious sense, they did not put up any armed resistance to the Romans, even during the Jewish uprising.

The situation is somewhat complicated, especially when one bears in mind some of the literature found around Qumran that appears to have originated with the Essenes. The Book of Jubilees is probably the most famous. The Book of Jubilees is, in some ways, an alternative to the Book of Genesis in the Old Testament. At the same time, although it details Creation and what followed, as Genesis also does, the Book of Jubilees has a distinctly Messianic message. It shows conclusively that those who believed in Jubilees definitely expected a Messiah to rise from within the House of Judah, and that ultimately the Messianic kingdom would lead to a new heaven and a new Earth. In other words, the Book of Jubilees seems to have more in common with developing Christianity than does the Book of Genesis.

The Essenes were fixated on two distinct principles, which they referred to as the 'Sons of Light' and the 'Sons of Darkness'. These are mentioned specifically in another series of Qumran documents known as the War Scroll. The War Scroll envisages a cataclysmic battle that will take place between the Sons of Light and the Sons of Darkness, and many historians have taken the Sons of Darkness to represent the occupying Romans. If this is true, it is never mentioned explicitly in the War Scroll, which goes into the most intricate detail regarding the way the Sons of Light should be dressed and arrayed, what battle tactics should be employed and what weapons should be used.

It is hard to look at what is known of the Essenes and *not* see the embryo of Christianity because so many of their beliefs and practices were almost identical to those of the earliest Christian aesthetes. Certainly Qumran and other Essene communities were flourishing around the time of Jesus and for a short period afterwards.

St Matthew, Angels and Scrolls

Going back for as long as it is possible to see, depictions of St Matthew always show him in association with an angel and with a scroll. Of course, angels are common in Christianity, but probably not as common as they are in the Book of Jubilees, which is replete with angels of all conceivable sorts. According to Jubilees, these heavenly beings were present at the very commencement of Creation and continued to be a potent force not just in the Christian religions but in Islam, Hinduism and Buddhism; in fact, most of the world religions made references to angels or spirits of light.

The near obsession with carved angels in Rosslyn Chapel seems to reflect the version of Creation portrayed in the Book of Jubilees and of course also amply displays the connection between St Matthew and angels. In addition, many of the angels in the Chapel carry open or closed scrolls. These angels can be seen in many of the master paintings of St Matthew by Rembrandt, Guido Reni, Giovanni Girolamo Salvodo and especially in *The Inspiration of St Matthew* by Caravaggio which appeared almost 80 years after the building of Rosslyn.

St Matthew is always portrayed as holding or writing in a book in the presence of angels who are often also bearing scrolls or pages of a book. In Rosslyn, we even have a corbel hierarchy classification of the angel lineage from seraphims to archangels and angels. This can be seen around the inside of the first window on the south wall. The angels start in the farthest corner of the east wall with a representation of the Shekinah, as an angel holding open the book, above the altar dedicated to St Matthew. Angels holding scrolls are also represented on every window ledge above and around the Lady Chapel. They pass around the Lady Chapel from the south wall across the tops of all the pillars and finish on the north wall with an angel holding a closed book, almost as if they are enclosing and protecting the Holy of Holies. Again, there could be a double meaning here. They could represent a book of hours of prayers, with one for each hour of the day. These were very popular in France in the early 15th century. Alternatively, the angels may be illustrating the importance of St Matthew's Gospel, reaffirming that it was given by God and Christ. On the other hand, the angels may be simply guarding the relics of St Matthew, just like the angels on top of the Ark of the Covenant.

As we mentioned earlier, we should perhaps bear in mind that, according to very strong early traditions, the Book of Matthew, when first composed, did not contain any reference to Jesus' birth and that all the other sections that Matthew's Gospel shares with the other Gospels were most likely added at a later date. It is highly likely that Matthew viewed Jesus as being the true Messiah – but as an Essene and so essentially therefore a Jewish way. No Messiah of the Jews, however powerful or successful, could ever be considered to be part of the Godhead, since in Judaism it is a cast-iron principle that God is 'one and indivisible'. This is a principle that was definitely also held by several early sects – the Ebionites and the Nazarenes to name only two – and of course we mentioned Ebionites specifically earlier in this book in Chapter Nine.

It is interesting to note that according to biblical scholars Matthew's Judeo-Christian Gospel was used as a base by many of the developing Christian sects that came out of Qumran, threads of which still exist today.

Evidence of Unusual Beliefs

This all preceded St Paul's interpretation of the Gospels; in fact, St Paul relates that his translation of Matthew's Gospel came from a Greek version, not the original Hebrew or Aramaic version. In truth, St Paul probably never even saw the original gospel of St Matthew.

Whilst Rosslyn Chapel carries a wealth of iconography, the carvings do not specifically reflect Jesus *as* the Son of God; there are a few representations of the Crucifixion and the Resurrection, but not within the Lady Chapel. Although the inner part of the Chapel does contain representations of the four Gospel writers, one in each corner, it certainly does not seem to display carvings related directly to St Paul or characters associated with the development of the Christian Church after its Jerusalem and Jewish origins were marginalized.

The portrayal of Jesus' life depicted in the first, unaltered version of St Matthew, which many contend was essentially a Hebrew and an Aramaic document, accords absolutely with what is displayed in the Chapel. As we showed at the start of this chapter, there is also a very definite emphasis on the story of the Temple in Jerusalem, and especially the Second Temple established by Zerubbabel and a priest called Joshua.

All of this evidence tends to indicate religious beliefs on the part of Earl William Sinclair, and most probably Sir Gilbert Haye, too, that did not accord fully with the dogma and practices of Roman Catholic Christianity at the time the Chapel was planned and completed. So much regarding Rosslyn Chapel also points to the fact that St Matthew was of supreme importance, not simply in terms of his position in the Christian story, but also because of the date upon which his feast day had been set – which, in turn, had a strong connection with the founding of the first two Jerusalem Temples.

As has always proved to be the case with regard to Rosslyn Chapel, the deeper one looks, the more skins the onion seems to have. Whether we will ever get to know the whole story of Rosslyn portrayed by its exquisite carvings is unlikely; however, we are well aware that the real treasure of Rosslyn is the knowledge that lies within these carved stones, a knowledge that has a direct link back through its close association with St Matthew to Qumran, St Matthew's original Aramaic gospel and even the Dead Sea Scrolls.

CHAPTER FOURTEEN

The Chapel
Then and Now

Here is very little in our wide and wonderful world, created by the hand of man, that stands alone and totally independent of its time and place. In the case of Rosslyn Chapel, all of those who research its origins, its possible purpose and its mysteries are inclined to use words such as 'original' or 'unique' when describing it. Perhaps such adjectives are appropriate because, as far as we are concerned, there is nothing exactly like Rosslyn Chapel to be found anywhere else on our vast planet. On the other hand, this Chapel, perched on the side of its steep glen, did not suddenly spring into existence of its own accord. Rather, it was planned and built at a specific date, by people who had particular beliefs and motivations. These people were subject to the social and religious norms of their time and also to the information available to them.

We need to remember that, like any historical structure, Rosslyn Chapel was not created old. There was a time when it stood new and pristine, when its carvings, both inside and out, were crisp and unaffected by the harsh Scottish climate and when the motivations of its builders made absolute sense – even if the building's secrets were not vouchsafed to just anyone.

In a way, Rosslyn Chapel has become a victim of its own success. It is really thanks to the revelations put forward by the authors Michael Baigent, Richard Leigh and Henry Lincoln in their massive blockbuster *The Holy Blood and the Holy Grail*[1] that the eventual, almost fanatical interest in the Chapel began. They picked up on the much earlier Victorian assertions that there had been some connection between Rosslyn Chapel and the infamous Knights Templar. The main thrust of their book was that Jesus had been married and had fathered children. This offspring had survived and proliferated, eventually creating a holy bloodline that had once flourished in Frankish Europe. This theory slotted into another story of mystery and intrigue – that of a previously little-known cleric from the south of France whose name was Bérenger Saunière. Living in the 19th century and the early part of the 20th, Saunière was said to have been in possession of proof that this holy bloodline had existed and that the Catholic Church had been complicit in the murder of its last representative king in medieval France.

The connections between Bérenger Saunière, his strange little parish of Rennes-le-Château and Rosslyn Chapel were always tenuous to say the least, but they were enough to start the modern procession of visitors from around the world. As a result, it was more or less inevitable that Rosslyn Chapel would be chosen for a location scene in the tremendously successful film *The Da Vinci Code*. The author Dan Brown had based much of his original novel of *The Da Vinci Code*[2] on the work of Baigent, Leigh and Lincoln and had included the Chapel in his plot. Once the building appeared on the big screen the floodgates were opened. For those of us who already loved the Chapel this proved to be a double-edged sword. On the one hand, it was now impossible to be alone in the building, as had been the case earlier, but the vast influx of visitors brought in more money, and, together with grants from Historic Scotland and from the European Union, this meant that the Chapel itself would eventually be fully restored.

✠ · ✠ · ✠

There is a phenomenon, which can often be noted in the case of subjects of mystery that capture the public imagination, which has no name but which is very obvious to those of us who work in the genre. As in the case of Bérenger Saunière and the village of Rennes-le-Château, once a few stones begin to roll down a popular hill, they soon become a veritable avalanche. There are now literally hundreds, if not thousands, of books about the supposed Rennes-le-Château mystery, and the vast majority merely review and regurgitate information that has appeared in dozens of previous books. If there ever was a genuine mystery associated with either Bérenger Saunière or Rennes-le-Château, it has now become irrevocably lost beneath an overlay of half-truth, conjecture and sheer fantasy.

From the start of our cooperation, we remained determined that we would not become part of such a scenario with regard to Rosslyn Chapel. Both for our first book and in the case of this one, we tried, wherever possible, to go back to original sources for all our information. This is because we see a great danger in relying heavily on what other people have written about the place – ultimately, such a strategy leads to a result similar to that achieved in the game of Chinese whispers that both of us played as children. For anyone not in the know, Chinese whispers involves a person whispering a phrase of a few words into the ear of a companion who then whispers what they have heard into the ear of someone else. After about ten or so such repetitions, the final person has to say out loud what they heard. The most famous example of the result comes from the First World War, where supposedly the phrase started out as 'Send reinforcements, we're going to advance' and ended up as 'Send three and fourpence, we're going to a dance.'

This is not to suggest that we have ignored folk tales and legends regarding the Chapel; on the contrary, John, being a local, has collected material like this throughout his 60-plus years on this planet. We both have enough experience as historical researchers to know that in many cases, if these are old enough, they might carry more than a grain of truth. After all, if it had not been for such a story, we would never have learned of the light box over the Chapel's large east window. But this is also a good case in question when it comes to illustrating our methods. Having been told that it was always suggested that a red light shone into the Chapel on St Matthew's Day, we set about trying to understand whether the story could be true, what the light looked like and from where it emanated. Ultimately, this led to our first-hand recognition of the light box – and also opened the door to many other astronomical discoveries.

There are many other carved codes within the chapel that need further research, like the apostles' corbel of the fourth arch on the southern side which shows a procession of holy men who we believe filled the empty niches round what we have come to call the new testament section of the Chapel; this is just one example of things we have registered, but don't yet fully understand.

Despite this, our investigation has run its course, for now. Though it is quite possible that other facts regarding the Chapel and its history may yet come to light, we are, for the moment, content that we have come as far as possible using the evidence at our disposal right now. We fully acknowledge that we have not yet, for example, obtained a translation of *all* the books that are known to have existed in the library of Sir William Sinclair. Who knows how much more these might tell us about the motivations that went into the planning and building of the Chapel? However, what we have done is to investigate these sources as much as we could and, as a result, have achieved a deeper understanding of the motives behind the Chapel's creation, as well as demonstrating to our readers how such information came about and why it all just happened to come together in one particular place at a specific point in time.

Working, as we have, mostly from original source material, we believe we have amassed a sizeable number of facts regarding the Chapel that cannot be disproved and which can only be repudiated as a result of the personal prejudices of other researchers and writers. This proved to be a slight problem after we published *Rosslyn Revealed*. There were at least a couple of agencies that clearly did not like or approve of some of our findings. It would serve no useful purpose to itemize what these agencies were, but we remain confident, without trying to turn the situation into a public battle, that in this book we have fully countered any of the supposed faults they found in our research. Suffice it to say that it probably won't matter how tight our evidence is, because there are some people who write books about Rosslyn Chapel from a starting point that is clearly intended to bolster an agenda they already have. This is something we have strenuously tried to avoid. We went where the evidence took us, with the result that some of our findings even surprised us.

Amongst the indisputable facts regarding Rosslyn Chapel we would place the following:

1. Rosslyn Chapel was planned and built so that its eastern end faced absolute true east. In one sense at least this was clearly undertaken because the patron saint of the church was St Matthew, whose feast day of 21 September is also the day of the autumn equinox, at which time the Sun rises due east. In order to achieve this feat the planners of the Chapel *could not* have been sticking to the calendar used almost universally at the time. They clearly knew that this calendar was 'wrong', and so they orientated the Chapel to face that part of east they *knew* was correct. This could not have been achieved without a significantly good understanding of astronomy. We have also shown clearly why it is called the Collegiate Chapel of St Matthew and, indeed, traced St Matthew's life and influence, which turned out to be a massive revelation.

2. Rosslyn Chapel has a very special light box built into the fabric of the building, immediately above the point of the east window. We can now show that this light box has always been present and that it was not a Victorian addition. The light box is no accident. It was deliberately created so that the rising Sun at dawn on the days of the

spring and autumn equinox would shine through the box, in which the rays of the Sun would be amplified and then passed as blood-red light into the body of the Chapel. Any bright celestial body that was in the right place on the horizon, such as the Moon or the planet Venus, would serve the same function.

3. We have been able to demonstrate that Rosslyn Chapel, as a building, is far more than a simple truncated part of an unfinished collegiate church. Because of its orientation, and particularly on account of its design at the eastern end, it was also intended to serve the purpose of a good, naked-eye astronomical observatory. It was supplied with specific, designated points at which observers could stand, using the provided pinnacles, together with features on the distant horizon (as foresights and backsights) to view a multitude of different astronomical happenings, from at least due north, through east, to due south, and actually very much further in each case. We have also shown that stone seats were supplied below the observatory, so that an equally spectacular, but slightly less accurate, view of astronomical events could be obtained by people other than those standing on the retrochoir roof.

Whilst some observers might suggest that the whole business of the astronomical observatory is no more than the hand of coincidence at work, we believe that our case is fully supported by the existence of the light box, which certainly could not have found its way into the Chapel by accident. We have also demonstrated, we believe for the first time, that those who planned the Chapel possessed all the knowledge they could possibly have needed to achieve what we remain convinced were deliberate objectives. This knowledge was included amongst the books of Sir William Sinclair.

4. We believe that only the most diehard sceptic could find fault with our conclusion that the east end of the Chapel, with its sumptuous, naturalistic carvings, owes its existence to the story of St Matthew and his visit to the city of Myrna or Smyrna. Every facet of the Gospel story is present (including the honey falling from above), and we see this as being one of our greatest achievements in the research we have undertaken. As a result, we virtually *insist* that this interpretation of the Chapel's carvings should be included in the talks given by guides in the building. After all, we have shown that the Freemasonic story of the Apprentice associated with the Chapel's most famous pillar is nothing more than a story, whereas the St Matthew connection could hardly be countered because it is supported by a mountain of evidence.

Whilst we think that the list above more than justifies the thousands of hours of research we have undertaken regarding Rosslyn Chapel, there are many other observations that we cannot conclusively prove, but which, on a balance of probabilities seem to be more than reasonable.

1. Rosslyn Chapel was at least partly built to be a deliberately created reliquary, intended to house the supposed skull of the Evangelist and disciple St Matthew,

which was brought from its former home in Brittany. Supporting this assumption, we have strong evidence that important people such as Mary of Guise were quite aware that *something* of deep importance, which was also a great secret, was housed in the Chapel. We have shown exactly why the presence of this priceless relic could never have been spoken about publicly, either before or after the Reformation. In addition, we have demonstrated that at various times the Chapel was considered safe enough to act as a reliquary for other religious relics such as the Black Rood. In other words, amongst those who were *in the know* it already had a reputation for serving such a purpose.

2. We remain convinced that those who built Rosslyn Chapel were not conventional Roman Catholic Christians as generally defined at the start of the 15th century. Sir William Sinclair, and almost certainly Sir Gilbert Haye, quite clearly had other agendas that might have been seen as suspect or even heretical when viewed by the hierarchy of the Church. It seems more than possible that they were the legatees of a very early form of Christianity directly linked to St Matthew and the Qumran scriptorium that had somehow survived and possibly evolved across many centuries, and had found its way to the far west of Europe.

3. We have equated these peculiar beliefs and actions with a group known as the Ebionites, who flourished across a wide area during the early days of Christianity. We fully appreciate that no knowledge of surviving Ebionites

is available to historians in a general sense much after the 5th century. However, we would point out that even if true Ebionites had existed beyond this period, they could hardly have acknowledged their beliefs, because if they had done so, they would have been arrested and undoubtedly executed for heresy. There is evidence to show that the secret belief system was still extant in the late 14th century.

4. Try as we may, we cannot dissuade ourselves that certain aspects of the beliefs and practices that seem to have underpinned the creation of Rosslyn Chapel had a commonality with Mithraism. Once again, there is no hard-and-fast evidence that Mithraism survived much beyond the 4th or 5th century, but just as the Ebionites could not have admitted to their beliefs when faced with the power of the Catholic Church, those committed to a belief in a form of Mithraism would have been in the same position. We have explained our reasoning, and the evidence that led to it, as thoroughly as we could. We admit that we may never know the truth of these matters, but it is also possible that they can be substantiated to a greater degree as more evidence emerges.

5. It seems highly likely to us that the legends connecting Rosslyn Chapel with Freemasonry are based upon solid fact. We were the first researchers to show connections between the Tironensians those mysterious builder-monks, and the Sinclairs of Rosslyn. It seems perfectly possible, and even likely, that the design, planning and even the building of Rosslyn Chapel owed a great deal to

the Tironensians, and particularly those at Kilwinning Abbey. Since the town of Kilwinning seems to be justified in its claims to be the true origin of Freemasonry (thanks to the existence of the abbey), it is not unlikely that Operative Freemasonry was brought to Rosslyn Chapel by the monks themselves, or else by secular freemasons (masons who specialized in cutting and carving Scottish freestone) who had been trained at Kilwinning.

In any case, as we have pointed out previously, it would have suited Sir William Sinclair to have a method through which he could obtain pledges of secrecy from those who helped him create the Chapel. If, as we have no doubt, the Chapel site contains hidden chambers and tunnels, the builders would have been well aware of their existence. Only by binding them with genuine and quite horrible oaths of secrecy could Sir William have been certain that his secrets would be kept safe. The traditions of developing freemasonry, like the knowledge contained within the guilds, would be passed on from father to son, and would eventually find their way into the community as a whole; but the secrets of what lay below the Chapel would undoubtedly have died with the first generation – except in the case of the Sinclair lords themselves.

6. When it comes to the legends that the bodies of generations of Sinclair lords are buried in secret chambers below Rosslyn Chapel, we remain convinced of the veracity of these stories. Whilst we could probably prove our point here, we have deliberately chosen not to do so, but we would point out that all the generations

of Sinclair lords had to be buried somewhere. There is no trace of their graves or tombs within the body of the Chapel or its environs. This alone must surely insist that they are elsewhere, sleeping away the centuries, dressed in their battle armour – but undoubtedly *without* the 12 Templar knights fancifully suggested by the later researcher, Father Hay.

7. It stands to reason that if the stories about the buried Sinclair lords are true, it is likely that tales about buried treasure may also be more than fanciful legends. We would point out that the skull of St Matthew, which disappeared from Brittany at precisely the time Rosslyn Chapel was being planned, has never resurfaced. We also have evidence that Sir Gilbert Haye had visited Pointe St-Mathieu very close to the time the relic disappeared, when he was on his way to Rosslyn. We consider it to be as good as proven that Rosslyn Chapel was built, at least in part, to be a reliquary for this relic.

8. Finally, there is the Black Rood (supposedly part of the True Cross) which had resided in Holyrood Abbey. This was a holy relic that was, and still is, of great significance to Scotland, and it is still missing. Scottish parliamentary records demonstrate that at one time it was vouchsafed to Rosslyn Chapel. Could this also be housed in the vaults below the Chapel? If so, then maybe at some time in the future it can once again take its rightful place at Holyrood, since it is of the utmost importance to the Scottish Nation.

Rosslyn Chapel was planned and built at the very dawn of the Age of Reason. It was conceived in the minds of people who were subject to the early but full forces of the knowledge that exploded across the Western World with the dawning of the Renaissance. This Renaissance world was beginning to move away from the world of enchantment that had prevailed between the Dark Ages and the start of the 15th century. The release of knowledge that had been acquired and fostered within the Muslim world – much of which owed its existence to the writers and thinkers of ancient Greece – was beginning to cause a revolution in the thinking of Western man. The Catholic Church had grown lax and corrupt, and at the same time its repressive regimes had stifled intellectual debate or the foster-ing of scientific principles that had been cherished in Greece countless centuries before. But once the box of knowledge, in terms of libraries of books, had been opened, even the most case-hardened pontiff, using the cruellest and most aggressive tactics at his disposal, could never close it again.

At this time the kingdom of Scotland stood in a unique position. It existed on the very fringes of Europe, about as far from Rome as it was possible for any Roman Catholic country to be at the time. As we have shown, Scotland was always different from most other countries in Europe. Independence had been fostered in its inhabitants as far back as history can relate. It was never fully subjugated by Rome. Many events, particularly the excommunication of Robert the Bruce, brought a freedom that allowed Scotland to develop an independent approach to religion, far removed from the strangling dogma and control of the Roman Church at the time. Scotland constantly fought off the machinations of its southern neighbour, England, and was ruled exclusively by kings who held their power by the *choice* of their subjects and not as a result of any supposed divine right.

Scotland always was, and still is, peopled by individuals who have their own opinions, their own traditions, their own liberties and their own forms of government. None of this is up for discussion, and neither is the insistence of Scotland that it should be the right of any of its children to have a good education, which from first to last will be free of charge – apart from the normal taxes paid by Scottish citizens. There is nothing new about this because, as we have seen, from the time universities came to Scotland, which was extremely early, *anyone* with sufficient intelligence could expect to work towards a degree and would not be charged for the privilege.

Anyone who knows little of Scotland and its history, and particularly those who view Scotland simply through the eyes of British historians, is never going to understand just how unique this country is. Rosslyn Chapel is a fitting example, probably *the most* fitting example of Scotland's unique nature. It is an unparalleled treasure which survived the vicissitudes of time against all the odds and which remains, sure and solid, as the 21st century runs its course.

It was never our intention to create the ultimate definitive book on Rosslyn Chapel. We are well aware that it might easily take another 50 years to fully understand all the carvings (almost as long as it took to create them). We have added our own interpretations to help explain what just a small number of the carvings represent, through our eyes and research. In John's case he wished to add further to the knowledge of the Chapel and the area of his birth and childhood. This we believe we have achieved by highlighting some of the main philosophies that gave reason to the Chapel's construction and incredible workmanship. There is still much work to do, but we both sincerely believe that we have laid the correct foundations for future researchers and interested individuals to build upon.

We consider ourselves to be supremely lucky to have been involved, even if only for moment, in the ongoing history of this most enigmatic structure. Long may the Chapel look out over its beautiful glen to the mournful hills beyond. Long may a free world benefit from the immense struggle of those who built Rosslyn Chapel, people who strove to push the bounds of human knowledge, whilst retaining the very best of what had gone before.

It is a slight shame that College hill house, the small building outside the Chapel wall, is no longer a public house. It would be fine to buy a dram there and to stand with it on the grass outside the Chapel's north entrance. Along with the ghost of Scotland's own bard, Rabbie Burns, we could lift our glass to toast the Chapel and all those who left us with such a wonderful legacy. In true Scottish fashion we would throw back the whisky with a cry of *Slaandjivaa!*

Rosslyn Chapel will always be a place of legend and mystery, and perhaps it is fitting that it is. But gradually it will betray its many secrets, which is also right because as the only linguistic inscription within Rosslyn Chapel ends:

The Truth Conquers All

APPENDIX

Extract from 'Acts and Martyrdom of St Matthew the Apostle'

From *Ante-Nicene Fathers, Volume 8*

A bout that time Matthew, the holy apostle and evangelist of Christ, was abiding in the mountain resting, and praying in his tunic and apostolic robes without sandals; and, behold, Jesus came to Matthew in the likeness of the infants who sing in paradise, and said to him: Peace to thee, Matthew! And Matthew having gazed upon Him, and not known who He was, said: Grace to thee, and peace, O child highly favoured! And why hast thou come hither to me, having left those who sing in paradise, and the delights there? Because here the place is desert; and what sort of a table I shall lay for thee, O child, I know not, because I have no bread nor oil in a jar. Moreover, even the winds are at rest, so as not to cast down from the trees to the ground anything for food; because, for the accomplishing of my fast of forty days, I, partaking only of the fruits falling by the movement of the winds, am glorifying my Jesus. Now, therefore, what shall I bring thee, beautiful boy? There is not even water near, that I may wash thy feet.

And the child said: Why sayest thou, O Matthew? Understand and know that good discourse is better than a calf, and words of meekness better than every herb of the field, and a sweet saying as the perfume of love, and cheerfulness of countenance better than feeding, and a pleasant look is as the appearance of sweetness. Understand, Matthew, and know that I am paradise, that I am the comforter, I am the power of the powers above, I the strength of those that restrain themselves, I the crown of the virgins, I the self-control of the once married, I the boast of the widowed, I the defence of the infants, I the foundation of the Church, I the kingdom of the bishops, I the glory of the presbyters, I the praise of the deacons. Be a man, and be strong, Matthew, in these words.

And Matthew said: The sight of thee hast altogether delighted me, O child; moreover also, thy words are full of life. For assuredly thy face shines more than the lightning, and thy words are altogether most sweet. And that indeed I saw thee in paradise when thou didst sing with the other infants who were killed in Bethlehem, I know right well; but how thou hast suddenly come hither, this altogether astonishes me. But I shall ask thee one thing, O child: that impious Herod, where is he? The child says to him: Since thou hast asked, hear his dwelling-place. He dwells, indeed, in Hades; and there has been prepared for him fire unquenchable, Gehenna without end, bubbling mire, worm that sleeps not, because he cut off three thousand infants, wishing to slay the child Jesus, the ancient of the ages; but of all these ages I am father. Now therefore, O Matthew, take this rod of mine, and go down from the mountain, and go into Myrna, the city of the man-eaters, and plant it by the gate of the church which thou and Andrew founded; and as soon as thou hast planted it, it shall be a tree, great and lofty and with many branches, and its branches shall extend to thirty cubits, and of each single branch the fruit shall be different both to the sight and the eating, and from the top of the tree shall flow down much honey; and from its root there shall come forth a great fountain, giving drink to this country round about, and in it creatures that swim and creep; and in it the man-eaters shall wash themselves, and eat of the fruit of the trees of the vine and of the honey; and their bodies shall be changed, and their forms shall be altered so as to be like those of other men; and they shall be ashamed of the nakedness of their body, and they shall put on clothing of the rams of the sheep, and they shall no longer eat unclean things; and there shall be to them fire in superabundance, preparing the sacrifices for offerings, and they shall bake their bread with fire; and they shall see each other in the likeness of the rest of men, and they shall acknowledge me, and glorify my Father who is in the heavens. Now therefore make haste, Matthew, and go down hence, because the departure from thy body through fire is at hand, and the crown of thy endurance.

And the child having said this, and given him the rod, was taken up into the heavens. And Matthew went down from the mountain, hastening to the city. And as he was about to enter into the city, there met him Fulvana the wife of the king, and his son Fulvanus and his wife Erva, who were possessed by an unclean spirit, and cried out shouting: Who has brought thee here again, Matthew? Or who has given thee the rod for our destruction? For we see also the child Jesus, the Son of God, who is with thee. Do not go then, O Matthew, to plant the rod for the food, and for the transformation of the man-eaters: for I have found what I shall do to thee. For since thou didst drive me out of this city, and prevent me from fulfilling my wishes among the man-eaters, behold, I will raise up against thee the king of this city, and he will burn thee alive. And Matthew, having laid his hands on each one of the demoniacs, put the demons to flight, and made the people whole; and they followed him.

And thus the affair being made manifest, Plato the bishop, having heard of the presence of the holy Apostle Matthew, met him with all the clergy; and having fallen to the ground, they kissed his feet. And Matthew raised them, and went with them into the church, and the child Jesus was also with him. And Matthew, having come to the gate of the church, stood upon a certain lofty and immoveable stone; and when the whole city ran together, especially the brethren who had believed, began to say: Men and women who appear in our sight, heretofore believing in the universe, but now knowing Him who has upheld and made the universe; until now worshipping the Satyr, and mocked by ten thousand false gods, but now through Jesus Christ acknowledging the one and only God, Lord, Judge; who have laid aside the immeasurable greatness of evil, and put on love, which is of like nature with affectionateness, towards men; once strangers to Christ, but now confessing Him Lord and God; formerly without form, but now trans-formed through Christ – behold, the staff which you see in my hand, which Jesus, in whom you have believed and will believe, gave me; perceive now what comes to pass through me, and acknowledge the riches of the greatness which He will this day make for you. For, behold, I shall plant this rod in this place, and it shall be a sign to your generations, and it shall become a tree, great and lofty and flourishing, and its fruit beautiful to the view and good to the sight; and the fragrance of perfumes shall come forth from it, and there shall be a vine twining round it, full of clusters; and from the top of it honey coming down, and every flying creature shall find covert in its branches; and a fountain of water shall come forth from the root of it, having swimming and creeping things, giving drink to all the country round about.

And having said this, and called upon the name of the Lord Jesus, he fixed his rod in the ground, and straightway it sprung up to one cubit; and the sight was strange and wonderful. For the rod having straightway shot up, increased in size, and grew into a great tree, as Matthew had said. And the apostle said: Go into the fountain and wash your bodies in it, and then thus partake both of the fruits of the tree, and of the vine and the honey, and drink of the fountain, and you shall be transformed in your likeness to that of men; and after that, having gone into the church, you will clearly recognise that you have believed in the living and true God. And having done all these things, they saw themselves changed into the likeness of Matthew; then, having thus gone into the church, they worshipped and glorified God. And when they had been changed, they knew that they were naked; and they ran in haste each to his own house to cover their nakedness, because they were ashamed.

And Matthew and Plato remained in the church spending the night, and glorifying God. And there remained also the king's wife, and his son and his wife, and they prayed the apostle to give them the seal in Christ. And Matthew gave orders to Plato; and he, having gone forth, baptized them in the water of the fountain of the tree, in the name of the Father, and the Son, and the Holy Ghost. And so thereafter, having gone into the church, they communicated in the holy mysteries of Christ; and they exulted and passed the night, they also along with the apostle, many others having also come with them; and all in the church sang the whole night, glorifying God.

Notes

Chapter One: The Chapel on the Glen

1. *The Hiram Key*, Christopher Knight and Robert Lomas, Arrow, 1996
2. *Rosslyn Revealed*, Alan Butler and John Ritchie, O Books, 2006

Chapter Six: A View to the East

1. During each year, the rising Sun appears to move up and down the horizon at dawn, from south to north and then back from north to south. The equinox marks the time, twice each year, when the Sun is halfway on its journey from summer to winter, or winter to summer. On the days of the equinoxes, the Sun rises due east and sets due west, and there are exactly 12 hours of day and 12 hours of night.
2. What this effectively means is that at midsummer the Sun rises at NE and sets at NW, whereas at midwinter the Sun rises at SE and sets at SW. In each case, the rising and setting points are midway between the cardinal points of the compass. In prehistoric times, to the avid sky-watchers of the British Isles this must have seemed like some sort of deep magic and would have made the latitude of Rosslyn Chapel very significant. It would also have made other astronomical observations based upon the rising and setting points of both the Sun and Moon that much easier.

Chapter Seven: The Blood-Red Light

1. *Uriel's Machine*, Christopher Knight and Robert Lomas, Arrow, 2000

2. *The Hiram Key*, Christopher Knight and Robert Lomas, Arrow, 1997

3. In Bronze Age times, Minoan Crete had outposts in Palestine. Eventually there was a huge cataclysm that severely damaged Crete around 1500 BC. As a result, waves of survivors found their way to Palestine, and they undoubtedly had a bearing on the cultures that were already living there – especially in terms of religion.

Chapter Eleven: In the Crypt

1. *The Goddess, the Grail and the Lodge*, Alan Butler, O Books, 2003

2. *The Hiram Key Revisited*, Christopher Knight and Alan Butler, Watkins, 2010

3. *Stellar Theology and Masonic Astronomy*, Robert Hewitt Brown, Kessinger Publishing (1882), 2010

4. By the time Hewitt Brown wrote his book in the 1880s, the spring equinox was actually occurring in Pisces, but astrologers, rather than astronomers, are somewhat 'fixed' in time, in that they always portray the spring equinox as being in Aries.

5. *Washington DC – City of the Goddess*, Alan Butler, Watkins Publishing, 2010

6. Most probably because he was not aware of it. A great deal more is known about Mithraism today than was the case in the 19th century. Since that time many more mithraea have been discovered and excavated.

Chapter Twelve: The View to the West

1. *The Temple and the Lodge*, Richard Leigh and Michael Baigent, Guild Publishing, 1989
2. *Before the Pyramids*, Christopher Knight and Alan Butler, Watkins Publishing, 2010
3. *City of the Goddess*, Alan Butler, Watkins Publishing, 2011
4. Astrology – the belief that the patterns formed by the heavens at any given point in time could have a part to play in the affairs of humanity, was still widely accepted at this time.
5. The only reason she was not called Liberty in this case was because of concern from the Southern States which were reliant on slavery and did not care for the implications of the goddess Liberty in this context.
6. The Megalithic matrix underpinning Washington DC is also fully explained at www.washingtondcschamberofse-crets.com

Chapter Thirteen: The Judaic Connections

1. *Solomon's Powerbrokers*, Christopher Knight and Alan Butler, Watkins, 2007
2. *The Secret Initiation of Jesus at Qumran*, Dr Robert Feather, Watkins, 2006

Chapter Fourteen: The Chapel Then and Now

1. *The Holy Blood and the Holy Grail*, Baigent, Leigh and Lincoln, Arrow Books, 1994
2. *The Da Vinci Code*, Dan Brown, Random House, 2003

Index

Figures are denoted with an *f'* and italicised page number e.g. Agnus Dei *188f*

Abif, Hiram 15, 181
'Acts and Martyrdom of St Matthew' 33
Adamson, Robert 11, 100, 115
Age of Reason 241
Agnus Dei 188, *188f*, 189
Albergati, Cardinal 48
Albert, Prince 3, 12, 128
alchemy 124
Alexander I, King 134
Alexander, James, third Earl of Rosslyn 12–13
Alexander the Great 218
Alexander's Journey to Paradise 218
allegories 177, 178, 181
America
  Capitol, legacy of the Freemasons 200
  Colonists 199–200
  Constitution of 201–2
  Freemasonry and 198, 199, 200, 214
  hotbed for Masonic bodies 198
  independence of British Colonies 198
  naval personnel survey 65
  revolutionary leaders 199
American Declaration of Independence 199–200, 200
American Intelligence Network 204
American War of Independence 198, 199
angels 4, 224–6
Angles 56
Ante-Nicene Fathers 28–9, 184, 245–50
Antiquities of the Jews 221
Antonine Wall 56
Apocrypha 28–9, 31, 32, 33
Apollo 107
Apprentice Pillar *see* St Matthew's Pillar
Aquarius 111, 168
Arbroath monastery 134
arches
  decorated 4
  pointed 139–40
  Romanesque 139
  stone cubes 5
Aries 168, 187, 188, 189
Aristotle 218

Ark of the Covenant 119, 209, 210
Armed Freedom 202
Arthur, King 146, 147–8
artisans 176
Ashtoreth 122–3
astronomical observatories
  Capitol 202
  Rosslyn Chapel 91–2, 100–4, 235
astronomy
  astronomical observatories 91–2, 100–4, 202, 235
  complex calculations 96–7
  Freemasonry and 180–1
  importance to Rosslyn Chapel 110
  observation of the Moon 89–90
  works in *MS Fairfax* 27, 95–6, 97
Auld Alliance 76–8
autumn equinox
  cornerstone of Capitol 201
  date of 92–4, 186, 234
  Jewish New Year 124
  Mysteries of Demeter 161
  view from Rosslyn Chapel 92, 99, 116

ba' 147
Baigent, Michael 198, 230
Balantrodoch 212
Baldwin II, King of Jerusalem 206
Balliol, John 76
Balmoral 128–9
Battle of Bannockburn 58, 212
Battle of Culloden 198
Battle of Dunbar 64, 66
Battle of Flodden 59
Battle of Teba 137
bees 52–3
beheading game 147–9
Benedictine foundation 36
Benedictine orders 130, 138
Bernard de Linton 138
Bernard of Clairvaux 132, 207
Bernard of Kilwinning 79
Bernard of Tiron 131–2, 136
Bible 123, 184

blood-red light 114, 120, 235
Bodleian Library 75, 95, 124
Boleyn, Anne 61
Book of Abel 213
Book of Esdras 217
Book of Genesis 223, 224
The Book of Jubilees 223–4, 225
Book of Matthew 226
Book of Revelation 189
books 71–3
Bosco, Johannes de Sacro 96
Boston 198
Bower, Walter 36
Brittany 36–7, 40
brotherhood 194
Brown, Dan 230–1
Brown, Robert Hewitt 180, 181, 189, 193
Bruce, Nancy 103–4
Bryce, David 13
Buckingham Palace 128
Buddhism 38
Buik of the Law of Arm's 175
The Buke of the Governaunce of Princes
    175
The Buke of tile 175
Burns, Robert 11–12

Caithness 7
calendars
    Gregorian calendar 94, 108
    Julian calendar 93, 96
    lunar 220
    solar 106–7, 220
calotypes 115
Calvinism 59
Camelot 148
canons 6
canopy 13–14, 91
Canterbury Cathedral 39, 105
Capitol
    astronomical observatory 202
    emulation of Solomon's Temple 203
    Freemasonic ceremony 201
    magnificent building 202
    Masonic lodges 201
    temple-like 202
Caravaggio 225
carvings, at Rosslyn Chapel 10, 13, 127,
    216–19
Cathedral of Salerno 37
Cathedral of St Matthew the Apostle 205
Catholic Church
    conflict with science 97
    demand for change 9
    differences with Culdean religion 135
    feast day of St Matthew 92

    monopoly in bookmaking 71
    opposition to wealth of 9, 60
    vandalism 9–10
Catholic Encyclopaedia 50
Celtic people
Celts
    Celtic Church 131, 134–5, 136–7
    farming community 153
    identity in Wales and Scotland 56
    religious ceremonies 151
    see also Culdees; Druids
Champagne 210–11
Charles I, King 64
Charles VII, King of France 35, 74
Chartres Cathedral 107, 133, 140, 209–10
choristers 6
Christianity
    attacks on 27
    calculation of date of Easter 93–4
    Celtic 134–5
    changes to Gospels 24
    comparison to Mithraism 172
    early 21, 22
    festivals 153
    incorporation of Mithraism 171–2
    relics, importance of 38
    Roman Empire and 22, 23
    vying with Mithras 160
Church Fathers 24, 160
Cistercians 131, 132, 133, 138, 141
City of the Goddess 200, 203
Clement V, Pope 207–8
close conjunction 118, 119, 120
College hill house 243
collegiate church 5–6
Colonies 196, 197, 198, 199
Columbia (formerly Liberty) 202, 202–3
communities 18
*Composed in Rosslyn Chapel During a
    Storm* 11
Comyn, John 211
Constantine 21, 22, 23
Constantinople 72
constellations 167
Constitution of the United States of
    America 201–2
Copford Church 105
Council of Nicaea 21, 22
Craft 179–80, 182, 184, 193–4
Crown of Thorns 42
Crucifixion 222
cruciform building 7
crypt
    burials, no evidence of 191
    lack of decoration 191
    qualification as mithraeum 191–2

Culdees
  differences with Catholic Church 135
  monks 136, 152
  religion 131
Cyrus the Great 218

The Da Vinci Code 1, 183, 230, 253
Darius I, King of Persia 217–18
David I, King 136, 212
De Anni Ratione 96
Dead Sea Scrolls 220
Declaration of Arbroath 78, 79–85,
  137–8, 200
dedication to saints 17–20
Delta of Enoch 209, 213
Desert Fathers 221–2
Devil 24, 160
Doonies 147
Douglas, Elizabeth 7
Dr Hemming 180
Druids 152
Duke of Brittany 47
Dupuis, Charles-François 186

Earl of Hereford 61–2
Earl of Leicester 37
east window *see* great east window
eastern end
  cruciform building 7
  facing the east 233
Ebionites 26, 27, 158, 159, 237–8
Edward I 'Hammer of the Scots' 57, 58
Ellipse Park 214
engineers 197
England
  culture and education 85–6
  fighting the Scottish 58–9, 64, 82–4,
    212
  industrialisation 128
  wars with France 76
English Civil War 64
Entered Apprentice 178
equinoxes 167–9
  see also autumn equinox; spring
    equinox
Erskine-Sinclair family 10, 63
Erskine-Sinclair, James Alexander 116
Essenes
  communities similar to Christian
    monasticism 221–2
  concepts of heaven and hell 223
  differences with other forms of
    Judaism 220
  early settlement 220
  life away from large cities 221
  marriage and chastity 222

reliance on solar calendar 220–1
  'Sons of Darkness' 224
  'Sons of Light' 224
  teachings of Jesus 222
  traditions of 221
Ethanim (now Tishri) 218, 219
Ethiopia 28
Evangelists 110, 185

Fairfax, Lord Thomas 95
Feast of Tabernacles 218, 219
Feather, Dr Robert 222, 223
Fellow Craft 178
feudalism 72
Florence 69, 70
'Floris and Blancheflour' 144
France, alliance with Scotland 76–8
Freemasonry
  allegorical themes 178, 181
  astronomy and 180–1, 193
  belief in deities 179–80
  brotherhood 194
  cosmology and 181
  Craft 179–80, 182, 184, 193–4
  formal existence at Rosslyn Chapel 192
  highest rank 179
  Knights Templar and 209
  lack of understanding by members
    174, 177, 194
  link with Rosslyn Chapel 183
  lodges 177–8, 180
  oaths 179
  Old Testament and 182
  origin of name 144
  planet Venus and 190
  popularity in the armed forces 197–8
  rise and development of 192–3
  ritual 181–2, 189
  role of tradition 178–9
  in Scotland *see* Scottish Freemasonry;
    Scottish Rite Freemasonry
  similarities with Mithraism 173, 175,
    181–2, 182–3
  society with secrets 177
  Solomon's Temple and 178
  survival and popularity of 194
  symbolism *see* symbolism in
    Freemasonry
  three degrees initiation 178
  Virgo, zodiac sign of 190
freestone masons 143–4
French Academy of Science 108
Friends of Rosslyn 204

Galileo 97
Gerard of Cremona 96

Gergy, Jean-Baptiste Languet de 108
gnomons 108
The Goddess, the Grail and the Lodge 179
Gospel of the Hebrews 28
Gospels
  changes to 24
  date and order 21, 22
  modification of 22–3
  St Matthew 21, 24–5, 26, 26–7, 222
Gothic architecture
  in Paris 140
  shape of arches 139
  style 4
  taller buildings 139–40
'The Grand Architect of the Universe'
  180, 193
Grand Lodge 178
Grand Lodge of England 177
Grand Lodge of Scotland 183
Grand Master of Freemasonry in
  Scotland 183
Grand Master of the Scottish Masons 12
Graves, Robert 151
'The Great Architect of the Universe' 180
Great Britain
  Celtic Christianity 134–5
  Germanic tribes 56
  Norman French, invasion of 57
  Romans, occupation by 55
  tribal groups 55
  see also England; Scotland; Wales
great east window
  detail of *117f*
  equinox experiment 113–14
  light box *113f*, 114–18
  pentagonal hole 112
  redesign of 115
  size of 111
  special light 112–13
Green Chapel 148, 150
Green Knight 148–9
Green Man 150–1, 154, 155
Gregorian calendar 94, 108
Gregory XIII, Pope 94, 153
Greyfriars Church 211
Guild Freemasonry 205
guilds 174–5, 175–6, 205
gypsies 154

Hadrian's Wall 56
Hay, Father Richard Augustine 64–5
Hay, Sir Gilbert
  books on guilds 175–6
  contacts of 74–5
  extensive libraries 192–3
  friendships with rulers 35

  knowledge of 215
  life of 34–6
  religious beliefs of 227
  tutor 36
Hay, Sir Gilbert (grandfather) 34
Hays of Errol 34
Hebrews *see* Judaism
Helios 163
Henry VIII 9, 40, 41, 61, 138
Highlanders 198
Hill, David 11, 100, 115
Hill of Belief 135
Hipparchus 164–5, 167
The Hiram Key 8, 121, 214
The Hiram Key Revisited 179
Historic Scotland 13, 66, 231
Holy Blessed One 123–4
The Holy Blood and the Holy Grail 230
Holy of Holies 119
Honorius II, Pope 206, 207
Hundred Years' War 40

iconography 105, 105–6
Industrial Revolution 197
initiation ceremonies 173
The Inspiration of St Matthew 225
*The International Standard Bible
  Encyclopaedia* 28
Inveresk 173
Ireland 55
Irenaeus
  outspoken critic 25
  Pauline Christian 25
  writings of 26
Iron Age 55, 151
Italy
  city-states 69, 70
  merchants, education of 72
  regions 69
  trade 69–70

James V, King 43
Jefferson, Thomas 199, 200
Jerusalem
  Church 25, 26
  Shekinah 119
  temples 178, 203, 218–19, 227–8
  treasures of 209–14
  see also Judaism
Jesus
  disciples 21
  life of 227
  Mithras and 159–60
  Nativity and 24, 26 158
  school attendance 220
  teachings of 222

Jewish New Year 124
The Jewish War 221
Joan of Navarre 211
John the Baptist 26, 188, 222
John the Evangelist 153
Josephus 218, 221, 223
Judaism
  Ark of the Covenant 119, 209, 210
  beliefs of 119
  Essenes 219–24
  Passover 189
  principle of 226
  return of Hebrews 218
  Shekinah 118–25
  uprising against the Romans 223
Julian calendar 93, 96
Julius Caesar 69
Jupiter 171

Kabbalah 123–5
Kelso monastery 134
Kilwinning 130, 178
Kilwinning Abbey 130, 143, 144, 213
King of the Revolutionary Colonists 199
Kirkwall 147
Knight, Christopher 8, 118, 119, 121, 200, 214
Knights Templar
  arrest and disbandment 207–8
  conspiracy theorists and 208
  excavation of ruins over Solomon's Temple 208–10
  founding of 206
  growth of 207
  Holy Knights 206
  presence in Scotland 212
  treasures 209–14
Knox, John 10

Lady Chapel 6f, 14–16
landowners 196
Leigh, Richard 198, 230
L'enfant, Pierre Charles 200
Leo 111, 168
Libertas 163
Liberty 202, 202–3
libraries
  Bodleian Library 95, 124 75
  expansion of 74–5
  Hay, Sir Gilbert 192–3
  National Library of Scotland 75
  Sinclair 75, 192–3, 233
  Vatican 50, 73
light box 113f, 114–18, 234–5
Lincoln, Henry 230
Lindisfarne 19

Lion 171
lodges 143, 177–8, 183, 198, 201
Lomas, Robert 8, 118, 119, 121, 214
London 128
Lorenzo 'the Magnificent' 72
Louis IX (later St Louis) 42
lower chapel *see* crypt
Lurianic Kabbalism 123

Maes Howe 109
Mail Bride 171
Malcolm III, King 136
Mars 171, 201
Mary of Guise 43–4, 61, 237
Mary, Queen of Scots 43, 61
masks 5
masons 143–4
Masons of Scotland 12
master craftsmen 127
Master Mason 178, 179
Medici, Cosimo de 70–1, 72
medieval cities 17–18
Megalithic structures
  construction of 87–8
  creation, mystery of 88
  Moon, observation of 89–90
  planning of 90
  site of Rosslyn Chapel 100
  Stonehenge 88, 109
  tracking the year 109
Megalithic Yard 203
Mercury 118, 170, 201
Messiah 224
Ministry of Works 13
miracles
  Evangelists and disciples 184–5
  Jesus 159
  Mithras 163, 185
  relics and 38–9
  St Matthew and 29, 44, 53, 184
mithraeums 172, 190, 191–2
Mithraism
  ability to remain secret 174
  beliefs of 162–3
  fraternal association 192–3
  guilds and 174–5
  initiation into 163, 170–1
  mystery religion 169–72
  origins of 161
  representational remains 162
  Roman soldiers and 162
  Rosslyn Chapel and 172–6, 238
  similarities with Freemasonry 173, 175, 192–3
  spread of 23
  survival of 175, 193

Mithras
  birth of 163, 163–4, 185
  moving the entire universe 168–9
  performing miracles 163, 185
  similarities with Jesus 159–60
  slaying the bull 163, 165, 187
  St Matthew's Pillar and 187–90
  zodiacs and 164–6
Molay, Jacques de 208
Monk, General 64
Moot Hill in Scone 135
Mount Moriah 209
Mount Zion 42
MS Fairfax 27, 95–6, 97
Munster, countess of 13
murdered apprentice, story of 14–16
Musselburgh 173
Myrna (now Izmir)
  account in the Apocrypha 29
  description of 29
  tree 29, 184–5
Mysteries of Demeter 161–2, 163, 190

National Library of Scotland 75
Nativity 24, 26, 158
New Testament 20, 21, 110, 184
New World 197–8
New Year celebrations 147, 148
Newgrange 109
Newton, Sir Isaac 124
Nicholas V, King 73
Nithsdale 7
Normans 18, 57
Notre Dame 4
Notre Dame Cathedral 42

Old Testament 110, 119–20, 182, 210,
  216–17
Orkney Islands 89, 146, 176

Palace of Westminster 128
Palestine 20, 26, 122
Papists 10
Paris, Gothic architecture 140
Passover 189
Pater 171
Pauline Christians 25, 26, 27
Payens, Hugues de 206, 212
Persia (now Iran) 160, 171, 186
Pharisees 221, 223
Philip IV, King of France 76, 207, 211
Phrygian cap 163, 202
Piccolomini, Enea Silvio de' (Pope Pius
  II)
  bond with Sir William Sinclair 49, 50
  early years 47–8

  elected as Pope 49–50
  illegitimate children 49
  personality and character 48–9
  visits Scotland 48
  writings 48
Piece Hall 188
Pilgrims 38, 39
pillars
  Ashtoreth 122–3
  magnificent pillar 14–16
  St Matthew's *see* St Matthew's pillar
Pisces 168, 187, 189
Pius, Emperor Antoninus 56
Pius II, Pope *see* Piccolomini, Enea
  Silvio de' 73
Pointe St-Mathieu 36, 40, 46
pointed arches 139, 140
The Poor Fellow-Soldiers of Christ and
  of the Temple of Solomon 206
Porphyry 166
prebendaries 6
Prince's Pillar *see* St Matthew's Pillar
Protestant Reformation
  growth of 9
  origins of 60
  in Scotland 137
Before the Pyramids 200, 203, 213

Quadrans Uetus 96
Qumran 220, 221, 222, 223

Raven 170
Ravenscraig 7
Reformation *see* Protestant
  Reformation
Regimental Lodges 198
relics
  dubious provenance 38
  income from 39
  miracles and 38–9
  open to public view 54
  St Matthew 43–4, 46–7
  value and importance of 9, 37–8
reliquaries
  architectural form 41
  Crown of Thorns 42
  increasingly ornate and precious
    41–2
  Rosslyn Chapel and 236–7, 240
  security for relics 40–1
  St Taurin 45
Rembrandt 225
Renaissance
  books 71–3
  desire for knowledge and
    education 70

liberalism 73
libraries 74-5
origins in Italy 69
reasons for 68-9
René of Anjou 35, 74
Reni, Guido 225
Rennes-le-Château 230, 231
retrochoir 4, 98-9, 99f, 100, 151
ritual in Freemasonry
clothing worn at ceremonies 189
lack of understanding by members 182
role of cosmology 181-2
River Jordan 220
Robert the Bruce 34, 58, 137, 211, 212
Roman Catholic Church *see* Catholic
Church
Roman Empire
Christianity and 22, 23
common religion 23
Mithraism and 162
punitive expeditions into Scotland
172-3
walls, building of 55-6
Romanesque 139
roof 4, 101-2, 103f
Roslin 1, 50
Ross, William and Carolyn 204
Rosslyn Castle 8, 10, 61, 75, 191-2, 213
Rosslyn Chapel
architectural style 5-6
astronomical observatory 91-2, 100-4,
235
building of 125-6, 141-2
celebration of the equinoxes 111
design of 97-9, 101-2, 141-2
Freemasonry and *see* Freemasonry
ground plan 2f
Latin phrase carved in stonework 217f
myths and tales 14-16
planning of 215-16
poor repairs 13
reverence to St Matthew 45-6, 51
seasonal nature of adornment 154-6
unusual design 44-5
victim of its own success 230
Rosslyn Chapel Trust 13
Rosslyn Glen 92, 173
Rosslyn Place 175-6
Rosslyn Revealed 16, 34, 158, 233
Rosslyn (Washington DC) 204, 213-14
Rouen 4
Rough Wooing 61
Royal Arch 181, 209

sacrificial victims 188-9
sacristy *see* crypt

Sadducees 221, 223
Saint-Denis Church 140
Saint-Mathieu de Fine-Terre abbey 36,
46-7
Saint-Sulpice Church 108
Sainte-Chapelle 42-3
saints, dedication to 17-20
Salvodo, Giovanni Girolamo 225
Saturn 171
Saunière, Bérenger 230
Scorpio 111, 168
Scotichronicon 36
Scotland
alliance with France 76-8
barbarism of the English 81-2
battle within the Church 134-7
centre of learning 85
Declaration of Arbroath 78, 79-85,
137-8
effects of the Renaissance 78
emigration 197
engineers 197
fighting the English 58-9, 64, 82-4, 212
freedom of the individual, belief in
79-85
high educational standards 129, 242
independence 195, 241-2
Industrial Revolution and 197
joining the armed forces 197
landowners 196
people forced from the land 196-7
population of 195-6
Protestant Reformation and 61, 137
repelling invaders 80-1
reputation for culture 129
resistance to the Romans 55-6
sheep farming 196
stone circles *see* Megalithic structures
tenant farmers 196
terrain 58
Tironensian Order *see* Tironensian
Order
treaties with France 76-7
Victorian English, view on 129
see also Scottish Freemasonry
Scottish Church 9
Scottish Crown 125
Scottish Freemasonry
first lodge 178
interest in Rosslyn Chapel 11-12
origins of 143
Scottish Reformation 138
Scottish Rite Freemasonry 179, 198, 199,
200, 213
Scottish Royal Crown 50
scrolls 220, 225

Second Temple 218, 219
The Secret Initiation of Jesus at Qumran 223
secret societies 174
secret vault 63–7
Secreta secretorum 175
Selkirk monastery 134
sheep farming 196
Shekinah 118–25
Shekinah Pillar 121, 122, 123
Shroud of Turin 54
signs of the zodiac *see* zodiac signs
Sinclair family
  association with Freemasonry 183, 184
  collectors of books 75
  encouraged Protestant services 10
  origin of family name 19
Sinclair, Henry 7
Sinclair, John 64
Sinclair, Simon 10
Sinclair, Sir James 11
Sinclair, Sir William (descendants)
  Freemasonry and 12, 183
  letter from Mary Guise 43–4
  skull of St Matthew 66
Sinclair, Sir William, Earl of Rosslyn
  Arthurian tales 150
  builder of Rosslyn Chapel 7, 19–20
  culture and education 85–6
  Freemasonry and 192
  grant to build Roslin 50
  knowledge of 215
  libraries 75, 192–3, 233
  oaths of secrecy 239
  religious beliefs of 227
  skull of St Matthew 46, 51, 59
  succession of son 49
  wealth 7, 46–7
  workers at Rosslyn Chapel 192, 239
Sir Gawain 148–9
Sir Gawain and the Green Knight 147–9
skull of St Matthew
  murdered apprentice tale 14–15
  in Rosslyn Chapel 51–2, 62, 65–6, 67
  in Saint-Mathieu de Fine-Terre abbey 36, 40, 43–4, 49, 51
  secrecy of 54, 59–62
  story of 36–7
Smyrna *see* Myrna
Soldier 171
Solomon, King 123, 158–9, 182
Solomon's Powerbrokers 219
Solomon's Temple 15, 119, 175, 178, 203, 214
Solway Firth 173
'Sons of Darkness' 224

'Sons of Light' 224
Southwell Cathedral 154
spring equinox
  date of 92
  Passover 189
  zodiac sign and 168, 187, 189, 252
St Andrew 81
St Anthony 18, 221
St Apollinaris 107–8
St Augustine Church 105
St Benedict 131, 222
St Catherine 19
St Clair 19
St Cuthbert 19
St Eligius 18
St John 110
St Luke 110
St Magnus Cathedral 176
St Margaret 136
St Mark 27, 110
St Mary's Church 106
St Matthew
  association with an angel 224–5
  dedication to 8–9, 19–20
  feast day 93, 94, 186
  Gospel of 24–5, 26–7, 222
  life of 28, 29
  miracles 119–20, 122, 218
  Myrna, story of 29, 184–5, 186
  patron saint of civil servants 205
  portrayal with a book 225
  representations of 20
  skull of *see* skull of St Matthew
  tax collector 20
St Matthew's Pillar
  bees 32–3
  Mithras and 187–90
  murdered apprentice, story of 14–15
  representation of Myrna tree 30–1, 33, 45
  style of 4–5, 30, 31
  text from Apocrypha 31, 32, 33
St Nicholas 18
St Paul 25, 26, 158, 205, 227
St Peter 205
St Taurin 45
St Thomas Becket 39
staff of life 31
standing stones *see* Megalithic structures
statues 10
Stellar Theology and Masonic Astronomy 180
stone circles *see* Megalithic structures
Stonehenge 88, 109
Stuart, Prince Charles Edward 199
Suger, Abbot 140

summer solstice 107
symbolism in Freemasonry
    importance of 177
    lack of understanding by members
        182
    planet Venus 190
    role of cosmology 181–2
    sacrificial lamb 189
    zodiac sign of Virgo 190
Synod of Whitby 135

Taurus 111, 165–6, 168
taxation 20–1
The Temple and the Lodge 198
Temple Mount 206
Temple village 212
Theorica Planetarum 96
Thom, Alexander 88–90
Tironensian Order
    abbeys 133
    ability to create 133
    building works in Scotland 134, 138
    choir monks 133
    development of building skills 133–4
    humility 138–9
    increase in number of abbeys 134
    origin of 130–1
    proficient in Gothic style 141
    Rosslyn Chapel and 142, 238–9
    settled in Scotland 136
    work and prayer 132
Tractatus de Sphaera 96
Troyes 206, 210–11
True Cross of Jesus (the Black Rood)
    58, 240
tunnels 65

Ulansey, David 164–5, 166
United Kingdom 57
University of St Andrews 34, 85
Uppies 147

Uranus 201
Uriel's Machine 119

Vatican 50
vault, secret 63–7
Venice 69, 70
Venus 118, 121–2, 171, 190, 201
Victoria, Queen 3, 12, 128
Victorian period
    English cities 128
    industrialisation 128
    writing about Rosslyn Chapel 127
Vikings 19
vines 14, 30
Virgin birth 24
Virgo 190, 201

Wales 56, 57
Waltham Abbey 106
Washington DC 200, 202, 203, 204,
    205–6
Washington, George 199, 201
Washington National Cathedral 205
western end
    baptistry 13
    masonry 7–8
Wilson, Meg 11
Wordsworth, William 3, 11

York Rite Freemasonry 198
Yyggdrasil (the Nordic Tree of life) 30

Zangwill, Israel 153–4
Zealots 223
Zerubbabel 218
zodiac signs
    churches and 105–6, 107
    equinoxes and 167–9
    Evangelists and 111
    Rosslyn Chapel and 110
    Zoroastrianism 160, 166